Have you ever sat down to learn to play bridge only to discover that you didn't even understand the language? Now at last you can teach yourself to play bridge the way it is meant to be played and amaze all those friends who have given you up as hopeless.

Terence Reese, a master of the art of bridge, has created the first easy-to-understand bridge book for beginners. Using a simple step-by-step program, illustrated with sample hands, he will teach you everything you need to know about:

The language of bridge

Constructive bidding

Defensive and competitive bidding

Tricks in a single suit

The play of notrump

The play in a suit contract

Scoring

And much, much more

Hailed by *The New York Times* as "the world's best bridge player," Terence Reese has represented Great Britain in all the world championship matches. Considered an expert in every kind of card game and gambling game, Reese is a master of backgammon as well. He has written more than fifty books, many of which have been widely translated.

MENTOR Guides to the Arts

**Buy them at your local
bookstore or use coupon
on last page for ordering.**

BEGIN BRIDGE WITH REESE

by

Terence Reese

A SIGNET BOOK

NEW AMERICAN LIBRARY

CONTENTS

INTRODUCTION

This is not the first book I have written for beginners, but the arrangement is new. By breaking up the game into small segments, I think I have made it easier to learn; and certainly it will be easier for you to find your way.

On the whole, I advise you not to read straight through, but to take the book in small parts. Make sure you thoroughly understand each section as you go along. When possible, test yourself. For example, suppose you have been reading about responses to opening bids of One. Deal the 52 cards into four hands, pick out a hand on which you would open, then consider how you would respond on each of the other three. Do this several times.

With one exception, the bidding style is that of "standard American." The exception is that I have advised a conventional Two Clubs for big hands. The old Forcing Two is too poor a method to be perpetuated and has long been abandoned by tournament players.

The starting-point of this book is simply that bridge is a game of cards. Later on, it will teach you quite enough to play and enjoy the game in any but expert company. And you will find that learning to play bridge is well worthwhile in several ways. You will have a hobby that never palls and a means of making friends wherever you go.

My wife, Alwyn, has kindly supervised the text, modestly observing that if she can understand it, anybody can.

Terence Reese

BEGIN BRIDGE
WITH REESE

Part I

HOW THE GAME IS PLAYED

When one is used to it, bridge seems an easy game to play—just to play, that is, not to play well. Yet, writing for beginners and making no assumptions, there is quite a lot to explain. When you have read this account of basic procedure, watch a game in progress and you will soon pick up the idea.

1. Meet the Pack

If you have decided to take up bridge, the odds are that you are already familiar with the standard pack, or deck, of 52 cards. You will know, then, that there are 13 cards in each suit. The suits are:

Spades, designated by the symbol ♠
Hearts, designated by the symbol ♡
Diamonds, designated by the symbol ◇
Clubs, designated by the symbol ♣

There are two stages in bridge, BIDDING and PLAY.* During the bidding the suits have a ranking order, as shown above: spades (the highest) and hearts (called the MAJOR suits), diamonds and clubs (the MINOR suits).

During the play the 13 cards in a suit rank as follows:

Ace, the highest card
King, next best
Queen
Jack
Ten

These cards are called HONORS. They are followed in rank by the low cards in numerical order:

9 8 7 6 5 4 3 2

Bridge is a game for four players, with two partners on each side. The partnerships may be prearranged, but if not, there is a DRAW or CUT for partners. For this purpose, the pack is spread face downwards and each player withdraws a card. The players who draw the two highest cards are partners against the other two. When two cards of the same rank are drawn, the rank of suit decides.

2. Beginning the Game

The player who has drawn the highest card has choice of seats and cards. He may, for politeness, consult his partner, saying, "Shall we sit this way and take the blue cards?" (It is usual, though not essential, to play with two packs of different colors, which are used for alternate deals.)

For literary convenience (these terms are not used at the table except in tournaments) the players are described by the points of the compass:

*Words that have a specialized meaning in bridge, when introduced for the first time, are printed in capitals.

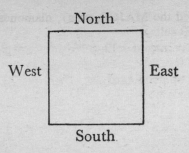

North

West   East

South.

Let us say that the player who has drawn the highest card has elected to sit South and take the blue cards. West will SHUFFLE (or MAKE) the pack. South will then pass it to his right for East to cut. East divides the pack into two portions, placing the top portion nearer South. South completes the cut and then deals clockwise, giving the first card to West, the second to North, and so forth. If the deal is correct, the last card will fall to South himself. Otherwise, there has been a misdeal and the same player must deal again after the cards have been shuffled and cut.

While South is dealing, his partner, North, shuffles the other (red) pack and places it on his right, next to West. When the first hand is over, West passes the red pack to South, who cuts for West to deal. Meanwhile East takes charge of the blue cards and shuffles them.

The position of the cards is always an indication of who is the dealer on the current hand. If the cards are on North's right, South is the dealer.

3. Tricks and Trumps

When the deal has been completed the players pick up their cards and SORT them into suits. The next stage is the bidding, but before you can understand the bidding you must have a general idea of what happens in the play.

Each player begins with 13 cards and plays one to each of 13 TRICKS. The basic object of the game is to score points by winning tricks. These are fixed rules of procedure:

• The first card played to a trick is the LEAD. The other players play to the trick in clockwise order. For example, if West leads, cards are played in turn by North, East and South.

• Each player must FOLLOW SUIT if he can, playing a card of the suit led. Failure to do so is a REVOKE, which carries heavy penalties.

• Most hands are played with one suit as TRUMP. (Whether there is to be a trump suit or not is determined by the bidding.) A player who has no card of the suit led may trump or RUFF (play a trump), and any trump beats any card of a PLAIN SUIT. If more than one trump is played, the highest trump wins the trick.

• Unless a trump is played, a trick is won by the highest card of the suit led. If a player has no card of the suit led and plays a card of a different suit (not the trump suit), this is called a DISCARD and has no power to win the trick.

• The player who has won the current trick leads to the next trick.

As an example, suppose that spades are trump. North leads ♡ J, and this is followed by ♡ Q, ♠ 6, ♠ 9. Here North's lead of the jack of hearts is topped

4

by the queen, but the queen is ruffed by South's 6 of spades. So far it is South's trick, but South's 6 of trumps is OVERRUFFED by West's 9. West wins the trick and leads to the next trick.

4. Declarer and Dummy

As a result of the bidding, one player on every hand becomes the DECLARER and his partner is DUMMY. The opponents are called the DEFENDERS.

The declarer is the player who first bid the DE-NOMINATION (a suit or notrump) in which the hand is played. This is the set-up when South is the declarer:

Dummy

Left-hand opponent   Right-hand opponent
(opening leader)

Declarer

Suppose that hearts are trump and South, who was the first player on his side to mention hearts, is the declarer. The OPENING LEAD is made by the defender on declarer's left, West. Dummy then puts down his cards, facing the declarer, like this:

♡	♣	♢	♠
K	6	A	J
10		8	9
6		5	7
5			4
			3

The trump suit, hearts in this case, is invariably placed on dummy's right. There is no prescribed order for the other suits, but it is usual to alternate the black and red suits.

Dummy takes no further part in the play, declarer playing the cards from both hands. Dummy can observe and has certain limited rights—he may, for example, warn the declarer against committing an offense such as revoking or leading from the wrong hand—but must not touch any card unless asked to do so and must not make any suggestions or comments. It is incorrect for the dummy to look at the cards of any other player, and if he does so he loses his rights.

Dummy is permitted to draw attention to an irregularity, such as a LEAD OUT OF TURN, and may state the appropriate Law, but if the irregularity is an offense by an opponent, any choice of penalty rests with the declarer.

5. The Play of a Hand at Notrump

You are ready now to follow the play of a complete hand. South is the declarer (as is usual in written diagrams) and there are no trumps.

```
              ♠ 9 7 4
              ♡ K 8 5 3
              ◇ A Q 7 5 4
              ♣ 6

  ♠ Q 10 8 6 2         ┌─────┐         ♠ A J 5
  ♡ J 9                │  N  │         ♡ Q 10 7 4
  ◇ J 6                │W   E│         ◇ 10 8 2
  ♣ Q 10 7 2           │  S  │         ♣ J 9 4
                       └─────┘
              ♠ K 3
              ♡ A 6 2
              ◇ K 9 3
              ♣ A K 8 5 3
```

A beginner may find it easier, at first, to set out actual cards on a table. However, that stage soon passes and much time is saved by becoming accustomed to written diagrams.

Note that the suits are set out in their ranking order of spades, hearts, diamonds, clubs.

West has to make the opening lead. He will probably attack with his longest suit, and we will say that he leads the 6 of spades. East wins this trick with the ace.

West, the partner of the player who has won the first trick for his side, GATHERS the four cards of the trick and lays them neatly face down. The trick is then said to be WON or TAKEN but any player may ask to see the cards again at any time before he or his partner has led or played to the next trick. Subsequent tricks won by the same side are placed across, or alongside, the first trick.

East leads the jack of spades at trick 2. South wins with the king and gathers the trick for his side. Now he plays diamonds, the suit most likely to produce extra tricks.

When both opponents follow to the king and ace of diamonds, South can be sure that the remaining cards of that suit will be winners. He can now count on making ten tricks altogether—five diamonds, the one spade he already has taken, two hearts, and two clubs.

6. The Play of a Hand with a Trump Suit

South is again the declarer and diamonds are trump.

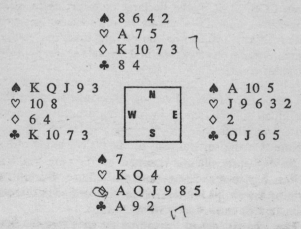

West leads the king of spades. East has no reason to OVERTAKE with the ace, so lets the king win the trick. West continues with a second spade, which South

8

ruffs. Here you see the advantage of playing with a long trump suit: at notrump South would have to suffer while the defense won the first five tricks in spades.

The declarer's next move is to draw two rounds of trumps. It would be foolish to leave low trumps at large, allowing the defenders to ruff side winners, such as the third round of hearts. In general, the declarer in a suit contract draws trumps early, unless there is a good reason to postpone that play.

The declarer now has ten tricks he can see "on top"—six diamonds, three hearts and one club. He can develop an extra trick quite easily by ruffing the third round of clubs. After drawing trumps (two rounds) he plays ace and another club, conceding the second round of clubs. He ruffs the third round and so makes eleven tricks, losing just the one spade and one club.

In the two examples here we have stated simply that there were no trumps or that diamonds were trump. As will appear in the next section, every hand is played in some CONTRACT, the declarer undertaking to make a specified number of tricks in a particular denomination. If the declarer on the present hand had undertaken to make eleven tricks in diamonds he would have made his contract.

7. How the Bidding Proceeds

Having observed what happens in the play, you will be better placed to understand the bidding. During the bidding the two sides contend to play with their chosen suit as trump or perhaps with no trumps.

The process is best explained by an example. Suppose that West is the dealer and the bidding goes:

South	West	North	East
—	pass	1 ♡	2 ♣
2 ◇	pass	2 ♡	pass
2NT	pass	3NT	pass
pass	pass		

West, having dealt, makes the first CALL. He is not obliged to make any positive bid, so he says "PASS."

North, who has some length in hearts, OPENS the bidding with "one heart." When naming his bid, a player states the number of tricks he proposes to make in excess of six (the term is not much used, but the first six tricks are technically the BOOK). Thus one heart is an undertaking to make seven tricks with hearts as trump.

East, who has a suit of clubs, OVERCALLS with two clubs. He must bid at the two level (at least) because clubs rank below hearts. (The order from high to low is notrump, spades, hearts, diamonds, clubs.)

South now joins in with a bid of two diamonds. With the opponents passing, North repeats his hearts, South ventures two notrump, and North RAISES to three notrump. When this is followed by three passes, the final contract is three notrump, played by South.

It may have occurred to you that North could have passed two notrump, leaving South with the easier task of making eight tricks. Certain contracts carry higher rewards, however, and that is why North advances freely to three notrump.

A THROW-IN. If all four players pass on the first round, the hand is "thrown in" and the deal passes to the next player.

8. Double, Redouble and Penalties

There are two additional calls beyond those we have mentioned. These are DOUBLE and REDOUBLE.

A side that bids to a certain level and fails to make the required number of tricks incurs a PENALTY. A player who judges that an opponent has bid beyond his limit may double. This has the effect of increasing the penalty should the double be left in and the player fail to make his contract.

South	west	North	East
1♠	2♣	dble	pass
pass	pass		

South, the dealer, opens with one spade and West overcalls with 2 clubs. North, who has values in clubs and has heard his partner open the bidding, promising some strength, judges that West will not be able to make eight tricks with clubs as trumps and so doubles, to increase the penalty.

This double does not affect the level of the bidding. East could RESCUE into, say, two diamonds; South could remove the double by making any SUFFICIENT BID (above the level of two clubs), but he could not redouble a bid that had been doubled by his partner. West could rescue himself into another suit or could redouble. On the present occasion the double is followed by three passes, so two clubs doubled becomes the final contract. If West makes two clubs, the rewards are increased; if he fails, the penalties are increased.

A player whose side has been doubled may redouble, raising the stakes still higher. This, too, does not alter the level of the bidding.

South	West	North	East
1♡	1♠	4 ♡	4♠
pass	pass	dble	redble
5♡	dble	pass	pass
pass			

Here North doubles East's four spades and East puts pressure on his opponents by redoubling. South, whose hand is not suited to defense, goes to five hearts and is doubled by West.

9. Part Score, Game and Slam

It is necessary now to say a word about the scoring. The various suits, and notrump, have a "trick value," as follows:

Notrump: first trick 40, subsequent tricks 30 each
Spades and hearts: each trick 30
Diamonds and clubs: each trick 20

If you bid and make a contract that is worth 100 points you score GAME. This is an important objective, because the first side to make two games wins the RUBBER, and this carries a big bonus.

The following contracts will score game because the trick score adds up to 100 points or more:

Three notrump (40 + 30 + 30) = 100
Four spades or four hearts (4 × 30) = 120
Five diamonds or five clubs (5 × 20) = 100

You may also achieve game by making two or more PART SCORES. For example, you may make one notrump (40) at one time and subsequently three clubs (60). This gives you game, provided the opponents have not made a game in the meanwhile. If that happens, the part score, as a step towards game, is canceled.

There is one other type of contract. A player who bids and makes a contract at the level of six is said to make a SMALL SLAM. A contract to make all thirteen tricks is a GRAND SLAM. There are substantial bonuses for slam contracts.

When a contract is doubled the trick score (such as 70 for two notrump) is multiplied by two, and when it is redoubled, by four. In the part score area there is an important distinction according to the level of the contract. If you double an opponent who has bid two diamonds and he makes it, he scores 80 (40 × 2), plus a small bonus. This is called a FREE DOUBLE, in the sense that opponents have not scored a game. But if you double them in two spades and they make it, you have doubled them into game, a minor tragedy.

10. Scoring Below the Line

WE	THEY

As you will see from the illustration on the left, a scoresheet for bridge has two columns and a heavy line across the middle. You enter your own scores on the left, those of your opponents on the right. It is advisable for all players to keep a scoresheet, because the state of the game has an important effect on the bidding.

The significance of the center line is this: the scores for contracts bid and made (such as 100 for three notrump) are entered BELOW THE LINE. All other scores are entered ABOVE THE LINE.

This procedure is not always followed according to the letter. If you bid two hearts and make four (10 tricks instead of 8), you enter 60 below and 60 above for the OVERTRICKS, calculated at the same score of 30 apiece. It would be wrong to enter this as 120 below, because that would give the impression that game had been made. On the other hand, if you bid three notrump and make four there is no objection to writing 130 below, instead of 100 below and 30 above, and this is invariably done.

When either side has scored a game, a line is drawn beneath it. This reminds the players that any part scores have been canceled, in so far as they contribute to the next game.

A side that has scored a game becomes VULNERABLE. From then on, until the rubber has been won, the penalties for failing to make a contract are increased, and so are certain bonuses.

The remaining details of the scoring are given in the next section, and a scoring table appears at the end of the book. It is not necessary for a learner to memorize all the scoring, which is derived from earlier forms of bridge and is illogical in some ways. Scoring becomes effortless with a little experience, because the same situations constantly recur.

11. Scoring Above the Line

BONUSES are scored above the line as follows:

Doubled and redoubled contracts made: There is a fixed bonus of 50 for all such contracts. Overtricks are well rewarded: not vulnerable, 100 for each overtrick when the contract has been doubled, 200 when it has been redoubled; vulnerable, 200 for each overtrick when doubled, 400 when redoubled.

Slam contracts made: For small slam, 500 not vulnerable, 750 vulnerable; for grand slam, 1000 not vulnerable, 1500 vulnerable.

Honors: For five honors (A K Q J 10) in the trump suit held by one player (whether declarer, dummy or a defender), or four aces at notrump, 150; for four honors in one hand, 100.

Rubber points: For a rubber won in two games, 700; for winning by the odd game of three, 500.

UNDERTRICKS: *Not vulnerable,* the penalties for failing to make a contract are:

Undoubled—50 for each undertrick.

Doubled—100 for the first undertrick, 200 for each subsequent undertrick.

Redoubled—200 for the first undertrick, 400 for each subsequent undertrick.

Vulnerable, the penalties are:

Undoubled—100 for each undertrick.

Doubled—200 for the first undertrick, 300 for each subsequent undertrick.

Redoubled—400 for the first undertrick, 600 for each subsequent undertrick.

UNFINISHED RUBBER: If for any reason a rubber cannot be finished, a side that is a game ahead scores a bonus of 300, and a side that has a part score in an unfinished game scores a bonus of 50.

12. A Specimen Rubber

WE	THEY
500 (7)	
750 (7)	
50 (4)	500 (6)
30 (2)	200 (1)
90 (2)	190 (3)
80 (4)	
100 (5)	
140 (7)	
1740	890

On the side is the scoresheet for a specimen rubber. The numbers in brackets (entered for the present purpose only) refer to the deal on which the score was recorded.

(1) You played five clubs doubled, down two, but held four honors for 100. You may enter this as a single figure in the opponents' column: 300 less 100 = 200.

(2) You played three hearts and made four—90 below and 30 above.

(3) Opponents bid three no-trump and made six, scoring 190 below and canceling your part score. A line is drawn beneath to show that game has been made.

(4) You played one notrump doubled and made it—80 below and 50 above.

(5) You played two diamonds and made five. This is strictly 40 below and 60 above, but as game has been made (thanks to your previous part score) you can enter it as 100 below.

(6) You played five diamonds doubled, down two = 500 loss.

(7) Happy omen, you played six clubs and made it with an overtrick. That is 140 below, and 750 for the small slam plus 500 for the rubber = 1250 above.

You have won the rubber by 1740 to 890, a difference of 850. If you were playing for stakes of so much per 100, this would be scored as 9 points, 50 or more rounding off to the next highest number.

Part II

CONSTRUCTIVE BIDDING

The term "constructive bidding" is used of the side that has opened the bidding. The subject will be discussed under five main headings:

■ Valuation and Opening Bids of One

■ Responding to Opening Bids of One

■ The Opener's First Rebid

■ Opening Bids of More than One

■ Other Bidding Situations

Bidding takes place before play, and this part of the game is therefore described first. However, the reasons for making a particular bid will not always be clear to a player who has no experience of what two hands are likely to achieve in combination. For a complete beginner, it may be a good idea to study first the early sections on play.

VALUATION AND OPENING
BIDS OF ONE

13. What Is Your Hand Worth?

A bridge hand may be strong in two ways: it may be strong DISTRIBUTIONALLY, or it may be strong in high cards. Compare these two hands:

(a) ♠ K Q 10 8 7 4 (b) ♠ K Q 8
    ♡ 5   ♡ A J 4
    ◇ Q J 10 6 4   ◇ K 10 7 3
    ♣ 3   ♣ A 9 5

Hand (a) is powerful in a way, but only if you find a FIT with your partner. You won't get far if he has a SINGLETON (one only) spade and a singleton diamond. If he has a blank in your suit, it is called a VOID.

Hand (b) is strong in high cards. It is, in fact, an ace and a king better than average. This is a simple calculation, for the average holding is one ace, one king, one queen, one jack.

The type that is strong in distribution cannot be valued with any accuracy until you know something about your partner's hand. The other type is easier to assess. The standard way of valuing the high-card strength is by "points." The POINT COUNT is a popular method of valuation whereby the high cards are assessed as follows:

Ace   = 4 points   Queen = 2 points
King = 3 points   Jack   = 1 point

Hand (a) above contains 5 points in spades, 3 in diamonds, total 8. Hand (b) contains 5 points in spades, 5 in hearts, 3 in diamonds, 4 in clubs, total 17.

Even at this early stage of your career it is well to understand that points are simply a shorthand way of summarizing high-card strength. Never let the point count *dictate* your bid. Make it your servant, not your master.

14. When to Open with One of a Suit

Bidding is a partnership enterprise in which the two partners aim to find the best contract on their combined hands. A player who opens with a bid of one does not merely indicate where his length lies but also says in effect, "I have a number of high cards which will be useful to you in any denomination you choose."

Opening bids of one spade, one heart, one diamond, or one club, cover a wide range of hands but have this much in common:

• A BIDDABLE SUIT. Any 5-card suit is biddable. A 4-card major should normally be at least Q J x x (x signifies any low card) or A 10 x x. An opening one club or one diamond may sometimes be bid on quite a weak suit, no better than x x x x or K x x.

• The hand should be about a king above average in terms of general strength. This does not mean that 13 points (the average is 10) is the minimum requirement. A suit such as A Q J 10 x x is a valuable asset and insurance against a MISFIT, because it does not require SUPPORT to be playable. This suit, with a king outside, would be a sound opening.

• The upper limit for a bid of one is normally about 20 points, but there are some hands with 21 points on which there is no better alternative.

21

Vulnerability, and position at the table (whether first, second, third, or fourth to speak), make a difference to some opening bids, but not to the majority.

Questions

As dealer, would you pass on the following hands, or would you open with a bid of one? Count the points always, but bear in mind that there are other factors to be considered.

1. ♠ K Q 8 7 5 ✓
   ♡ A J 10 5
   ◇ J 6 4
   ♣ 3

2. ♠ 7 6
   ♡ K J 10 7 5 3
   ◇ 5
   ♣ A 8 6 3

3. ♠ A 8 6 5
   ♡ 6 2
   ◇ J 9 4
   ✓ ♣ A K 5 2

4. ♠ A Q 8 4
   ♡ 5 3 2
   ◇ J 7 6 4
   ♣ K Q

Answers

1. Certainly you should open one spade. It is an advantage to hold both major suits, as game is easier to make in a major than a minor. Also, the combination of A J 10 in hearts is worth more than the 5 points assigned to it.

2. This is not a sound opening in first or second hand, but many players would open one heart in third position for tactical reasons. By opening, you may obstruct the opponents and you indicate a good line of attack should your partner become the opening leader.

3. Not a powerful hand, but it contains three QUICK TRICKS (the ace and the A K), and these will pull their weight if partner has a long suit anywhere. Open one club.

22

4. This would be a poor opening for several reasons. It is a disadvantage to have 5 points wrapped up in the K Q of clubs (called a DOUBLETON).

15. When There Is a Choice of Suits

These are general principles:

• With two 5-card suits, open the higher-ranking except when the suits are spades and clubs. Then one club leaves more space for partner's reply.

• With two 4-card suits open the higher-ranking when the suits are adjacent (such as spades and hearts), but usually the lower-ranking when there is an interval between them.

• With suits of unequal length, normally open the longer.

Questions

Which suit would you open on the following hands?

1. ♠ 5
   ♥ K 9 7 4 2
   ♦ A K J 7 3
   ♣ Q 6

2. ♠ K 5
   ♥ A K 10 2
   ♦ 6 4
   ♣ K 9 7 5 3

3. ♠ 8 3
   ♥ A J 6 4
   ♦ K Q 10 6
   ♣ Q 8 3

4. ♠ A Q 8 6
   ♥ 9 5
   ♦ A 10 6 2
   ♣ K 7 4

Answers

1. Open one heart. Do not be influenced by the fact that the diamonds are stronger. The bidding develops more smoothly if you begin with the higher suit, and in the end it is the length, not the strength, of the trump suit that counts.

2. Open the longer suit, one club.

3. Open one heart. You are then prepared for a RESPONSE in either spades or clubs: over one spade by your partner you can bid one notrump, and over two clubs, two diamonds.

4. Open one diamond. If partner responds in your weakest suit, one heart, you can rebid one spade, keeping the bidding at a low and safe level.

16. The Opening Bid on Balanced Hands

On a BALANCED hand, containing no singleton and no long suit, it is natural to open one notrump, provided the hand falls into the appropriate range. Beginners are advised to use a strong notrump of 16–18, but it must be mentioned that different styles are playable. Some play a weak notrump of 12–14 in certain circumstances.

The commonest distribution for a notrump opening is 4–3–3–3 or 4–4–3–2, but the bid is often made on 5–3–3–2, especially when the 5-card suit is a minor.

One consequence of playing a 16–18 notrump is that a PREPARED bid in a short minor suit is often necessary on hands that are too weak—or, occasionally, too strong—for the notrump opening.

Questions

What would you open on the following hands?

1. ♠ Q 6
   ♡ A 10 4
   ♦ A J 7 5 2
   ♣ K Q 8

2. ♠ K 8 6 2
   ♡ 8 7 3
   ♦ K J 4
   ♣ A Q 5

3. ♠ K 10 3
   ♡ A Q 8 2
   ♦ A Q 7
   ♣ A 10 9

4. ♠ K Q 6 4
   ♡ 5 2
   ♦ A K 6 2
   ♣ A 4 3

Answers

1. It would not be a mistake to open one diamond, but one notrump is more descriptive. You give a picture of the strength and character in one bid.

2. You would not get bad marks from the author if you elected to pass this flat 13-pointer, especially when vulnerable. However, most players are programmed to open on any hand containing 13 points. The best opening is one club.

3. This 19-point hand with good INTERMEDIATES (10s and 9s) is above the limit for one notrump. Prefer one club or one diamond to one heart.

4. This hand is within the range, but the texture is poor for one notrump. Open one diamond.

RESPONDING TO OPENING BIDS OF ONE

17. A Preliminary View of Responses

The partner of the opening bidder is called the RESPONDER, and the first response is one of the most critical areas in the game. This is the general system:

The weakest call

A pass; this is generally correct on hands with less than 6 points unless they contain a fair suit that can be bid at the level of one or fair support for partner's suit.

Limited bids

One notrump is a modest reply, with a range of about 6 to 9. A single raise, one heart—two hearts, also denotes limited values.

Bids of variable strength

A new suit at minimum level, one diamond—one heart, or one spade—two clubs, has a wide range.

Strong bids

Responses of two notrump, or a double raise, one spade—three spades, are forcing.

Forcing bids

A jump in a new suit, one club—two spades, or one spade—three diamonds, is forcing to game and unlimited.

18. The Response on a Weak Hand

The opening bid of one in a suit may be strong, as we have noted, but it is not FORCING. Responder should normally pass when there is little prospect of making a game.

A flat 6 points is on the borderline. It is true that if the opener has a maximum 21 points, or if he has two long suits in a good hand, there may be a game somewhere. However, it is wrong to proceed on that assumption. Suppose the opener has 19, which is well above average: game will still be doubtful with a combined 25 and no long suit. (Generally 26 points is a safe standard for game in notrump.)

The decision is more awkward when you hold a weak but unbalanced hand. For example, partner opens one spade and you hold:

♠ —
♡ Q 8 7 5 3 2
◇ J 7 5 2
♣ 9 4 3

It may well be that two hearts is a better contract than one spade, but you will not be able to stop there. The wise course is to pass and not risk a calamity.

You may, however, respond at the *one* level on a hand such as this. For tactical reasons it is undesirable to give the opponents a free run by passing and the response in a suit at the one level is not so dangerous.

Questions

1. Partner has opened one diamond. What action do you take on the following hands?

(a)
♠ Q 8 6 3
♥ J 9 5 2
♦ 4
♣ 10 8 7 4

(b)
♠ K J 8 5 2
♥ 4 2
♦ 8 5 3
♣ 9 7 4

2. Partner has opened one heart. What action do you take on the following hands:

(c)
♠ Q 6 3
♥ 8 4
♦ K 8 7 5 2
♣ 10 6 2

(d)
♠ 9 6
♥ 4
♦ A 8 3
♣ J 10 8 7 5 3 2

Answers

1. (a) One diamond may not be a good spot, but if you seek to improve with one heart (correctly choosing the lower suit and leaving room for partner to bid one spade) the bidding may go out of control. It is wiser to pass. Quite possibly, the fourth player will REOPEN, and you have fair defense against anything the opponents may call.

(b) Though you have less than partner will expect, it is not too dangerous to respond one spade. One advantage is that you make it more difficult for the opponents to contest in hearts.

2. (c) You must pass. You are under strength for one notrump and cannot contemplate a response of two diamonds.

(d) Again, two clubs would be unsound and you must pass. You may have an opportunity later on.

19. The Response of One Notrump

This very common reply has a range of about 6 to 9. Over one club the limits are slightly higher, more like 7 to 10.

It is *not* necessary to have notrump distribution. Fair values are needed for a response at the two level, so one notrump is sometimes the best answer on a hand with unbalanced distribution such as 6–3–3–1.

Questions

1. Partner has opened one heart. What do you respond on the following hands?

(a)   ♠ J 5 4
       ♡ 3
       ◇ K 9 6 2
       ♣ Q J 7 3 2

(b)   ♠ 10 8 7 3
       ♡ K 8 4
       ◇ Q J 3
       ♣ Q 10 5

2. Partner has opened one club. What do you respond on the following hands?

(c)   ♠ Q 8 5
       ♡ A 8 3
       ◇ 9 7 4 2
       ♣ 10 8 5

(d)   ♠ K 8 6
       ♡ A 10 5
       ◇ 7 4 2
       ♣ K 8 5 3

Answers

1. (a) Respond one notrump, not two clubs.

(b) While it is usually correct to respond in a 4-card major, the weakness of the suit and the balanced distribution point clearly to one notrump.

2. (c) Here one diamond is preferable to one no-

29

trump. Over one club, remember, the range for the no-trump response is higher than over one of a major suit. (It would not be far wrong to pass, but one is always reluctant to leave partner in one club, which is often bid with a short suit of only 3 cards.)

(d) You have support for clubs, but the hand is best expressed by a response of one notrump.

20. A Single Raise

Like one notrump, a single raise of partner's suit is a limited response. The requirements are:

• Trump support. It is never right to raise a minor suit on less than four cards, because a more constructive response must be available; but a major suit may be supported on three cards when there is a short suit outside (see next paragraph).

• A "ruffing value"; that is to say, a shortage in a side suit, so that extra tricks can be made by ruffing. A void or singleton is obviously best for this purpose, but a doubleton also qualifies.

• An upper limit of about 10 points. There is no lower limit because we are concerned now with "playing tricks."

Questions

1. Partner has opened one spade. What action do you take on the following hands?

(a) ♠ J 8 5
♡ 4
◇ 10 8 5 3
♣ A 9 7 5 2

(b) ♠ Q 10 4 3
♡ 9 7 5 2
◇ 3
♣ J 7 4 2

30

2. Partner has opened one diamond. What action do you take on the following hands?

(c)   ♠ 9 7
     ♡ J 9 6 4
     ♢ A 8 3 2
     ♣ K 7 5

(d)   ♠ Q 8 4 3
     ♡ 5 3
     ♢ K 9 7 6 2
     ♣ 6 4

Answers

1. (a) Although the trump support is moderate, two spades is the best answer.

   (b) This is a poor hand, but for tactical reasons it is right to raise to two spades.

2. (c) A raise to two diamonds would not be a mistake on the values held, but a response of one heart is more constructive.

   (d) As the preceding answer shows, it is not usual to suppress a 4-card major, but here two diamonds is the sensible call.

21. Responding in a New Suit

A response in a new suit, according to a universal convention, is forcing for one round. (This does not apply if the responder has previously passed.)

A response at the level of one, as we have seen, may be quite weak, not more than 4 or 5 points. It may also be strong—at least 15 points.

A response at the level of two promises fair values. The minimum with only a fair suit is about 9 points. With a long, rebiddable suit, you may respond on 7 or 8 points.

When two suits are held, the general rules are:

• With suits of unequal length bid the longer, unless this would involve an unsound response at the level of two.

• With suits of equal length, bid the higher-ranking when both contain five cards, but the lower-ranking of two 4-card suits.

Questions

1. Partner has opened one heart. What is your response on the following hands?

(a) ♠ K 9 6 3
   ♡ 7 2
   ◊ K J 7 5 4
   ♣ 6 4

(b) ♠ 6
   ♡ 4 2
   ◊ J 5 3 2
   ♣ A Q 10 8 7 4

2. Partner has opened one club. What is your response on the following hands?

(c) ♠ A Q 10 2
   ♡ 8 4
   ◊ Q 9 7 5
   ♣ 7 5 2

(d) ♠ K Q 6 3
   ♡ K 10 8 5 3
   ◊ A 4
   ♣ 7 2

Answers

1. (a) As you lack the values for a response at the two level, you must respond one spade.

(b) You can hardly respond one notrump with a singleton spade, so the choice is between a pass and two clubs. The strong suit justifies a response of two clubs.

2. (c) Respond one diamond, the lower of two 4-card suits.

(d) Bid the longer suit, one heart.

32

22. Two Notrump and a Double Raise

These two responses are usually played as forcing to game in effect.

A response of two notrump indicates a balanced hand in the range of about 13 to 15. A double raise, such as one heart—three hearts, is forcing and responder's hand will normally contain a minimum of about 10 points in high cards and, of course, good trump support.

Questions

1. Partner has opened one heart. What would you respond on the following hands?

(a)   ♠ K 9 5
       ♡ J 7 4
       ◇ A J 8 5
       ♣ K 9 2

(b)   ♠ 5
       ♡ K J 8 4
       ◇ A 9 7 6 3
       ♣ Q 6 2

2. Partner has opened one diamond. What would you respond on the following hands?

(c)   ♠ K 8 4
       ♡ J 10 7 6
       ◇ A 8 7
       ♣ A Q 5

(d)   ♠ J 6
       ♡ K 9 2
       ◇ K Q 6 3
       ♣ A 10 5 2

Answers

1. (a) You are slightly below strength for a direct two notrump. For the moment, respond two diamonds.

   (b) This is in the lower range for a forcing re-

sponse of three hearts. In playing terms the hand is
worth a raise to four, but this, as will appear in the
next section, is actually a weaker response.

2. (c) With a balanced 14, respond two notrump.

(d) This hand is suitable for a forcing raise to
three diamonds.

23. Three Notrump and a Raise to Game

Since you are playing the upper limit for a forcing
two notrump as 15, three notrump suggests a balanced
16 to 17.

A direct raise to game, one spade—four spades,
promises strong trump support but not more than
about 10 points in high cards. This is in principle a
SHUT-OUT bid.

Questions

Partner has opened one heart. What do you respond
on the following hands?

1. ♠ 8 4
   ♡ Q 10 7 6 4 3
   ◊ 5
   ♣ A 9 6 4

2. ♠ Q 8
   ♡ K 10 7 4 2
   ◊ A 9 5 3
   ♣ 4 3

3. ♠ K J 5
   ♡ K 4 3
   ◊ K 7 5 2
   ♣ A Q 8

Answers

1. An obvious raise to four hearts.
2. Raise to four hearts. The hand is close to maximum, in terms of high cards, for this response.
3. With a balanced 16, respond three notrump.

24. A Jump in a New Suit

A jump in a new suit, one heart—two spades, or one spade—three clubs, is forcing to game and of unlimited strength. This type of bid is called a JUMP SHIFT.

It is right to force when you hold either
● a balanced hand too good for a direct three notrump, or
● exceptionally strong support for partner's suit, or
● a good hand with a powerful suit of your own.

When several final contracts are possible, a gradual approach may be better. For example, partner opens one heart and you hold:

♠ 7 3
♡ Q 6
◇ A Q J 5 2
♣ A K 8 4

Certainly with 16 points you intend to finish in game at least, perhaps slam, but you will need *time* to express all your features. Respond simply two diamonds. (Note that only the *single* jump is strong: a *double* jump, one diamond—three hearts, is a weak bid on a long suit, such as K J 10 9 8 x x.)

35

Questions

Partner has opened one spade. What do you respond on the following hands?

1. ♠ 5 2
   ♡ A K J 10 9 7
   ◊ A K 10
   ♣ 6-3 *15*

2. ♠ 9 3
   ♡ A Q J 4
   ◊ K J 9 2
   ♣ A Q 7 *16*

3. ♠ K Q 10 4
   ♡ A 10 5 2
   ◊ 4
   ♣ A J 6 3 *14*

Answers

1. Force with three hearts and follow with four hearts on the next round.
2. Force with three diamonds and, if space allows, bid three notrump on the next round.
3. Force with three clubs and follow with four spades.

THE OPENER'S FIRST REBID

25. A Preliminary View of Opener's Rebids

After the first response the opener makes his first REBID. This completes the groundwork of bidding.

Rebids, like responses, fall into certain categories.

The opener may pass a response that is not forcing, such as one notrump. He may rebid in a way that limits his hand, make a rebid of variable strength, an encouraging rebid, or a forcing rebid.

Limited rebids

A repeat of opener's suit at minimum level, in a sequence such as one heart—two clubs—two hearts, is consistent with a minimum opening. A single raise of responder's suit is also a rebid in the lower range. So is a rebid of one notrump.

Rebids of variable strength

A simple change of suit, one diamond—one heart—one spade, or one heart—two clubs—two diamonds, may be made on a minimum hand, or may be much stronger.

Encouraging rebids

A rebid of two notrump, when partner has responded at the level of two, is constructive. A jump to two notrump, or a double raise of responder's suit, is a strong invitation to game.

Forcing rebids

A jump in a new suit is forcing to game and will usually contain a fit in responder's suit.

26. Opener's Rebid over One Notrump or a Single Raise

When the bidding begins one heart—one notrump, or one heart—two hearts, the responder's hand is known to be limited. To try for game, the opener needs either unusual distribution or about an ace beyond a minimum opening bid.

You hold:

♠ 5 2
♡ A K 9 6 4
◇ K J 3
♣ A 6 2

You open one heart and partner responds one no-trump. Now, what are the prospects of game in no-trump? Partner's range is from 6 to 9. You hold 15. As you need about 25 for game to be a fair proposition, you should be content to play in one notrump. To raise to two notrump you need about 17 unless you have the benefit of a long suit which you expect to run.

Suppose, next, that partner had raised one heart to two hearts. Again, you should be content to make a safe part score. But transfer a spade to one of the minor suits, giving you 5–4–3–1 distribution, and you have a hand well worth a try for game. A new suit, following a raise, is unconditionally forcing. Partner will go to four hearts if he has anything better than a moderate raise.

Questions

1. You open one spade and partner responds one notrump. What do you rebid on the following hands?

(a)   ♠ K 9 7 5 2   (b)   ♠ A K J 7 6 2
      ♡ A Q 4   ♡ A 5 4
      ◇ K 8 4 2   ◇ K 6 2
      ♣ J   ♣ 4

2. You open one spade and partner raises to two spades. What do you rebid on the following hands?

38

(c) ♠ K J 8 6 4   (d) ♠ K Q 9 4
   ♡ A 4   ♡ A Q 4 3
   ◇ A K 10 5 2   ◇ 7 5
   ♣ 3   15   ♣ A J 2

Answers

1. (a) You might fall on your feet in two diamonds, which would not be in any way forcing, but it is better to stay at the one level in one notrump. Partner may well have length in clubs. To take out into two spades with such a poor suit would be horrible.

(b) The 6-card suit makes a big difference. You can jump to three spades, inviting game.

2. (c) There will probably be a good play for four spades and you should bid this at once.

(d) You have 16, but no 5-card suit. A game is not impossible, but on balance you should pass and be content with a safe part score.

27. Opener's Rebid after a Response at the One Level

In a sequence such as one diamond—one spade, responder may be quite weak, and an opener's rebids are based on that assumption.

A rebid of one notrump suggests about 13 to 15. For a jump to two notrump the range is about 18–19.

A new suit at the level of one is consistent with a minimum opening, and a new suit at the level of two, one heart—one spade—two clubs, may also be quite weak in high cards. But a new suit of higher rank than your first suit, one club—one spade—two hearts, promises at least a king better than a minimum opening. The sequence (when you bid a higher suit at the two level on the second round) is called a REVERSE.

39

Questions

You open one diamond and partner responds one spade. What do you rebid on the following hands?

1. ♠ A J 4 2
    ♡ 5
    ◇ A K 8 6 4
    ♣ K 6 4

2. ♠ A 4
    ♡ A Q 6 4
    ◇ K J 10 7 3
    ♣ 5 2

3. ♠ Q 8 5
    ♡ 3
    ◇ A J 7 6 4
    ♣ A J 9 3

Answers

1. You are worth a double raise to three spades, but no more. Remember that responder may be quite weak.

2. You are not strong enough to reverse, so you must simply rebid the diamonds.

3. Raise to two spades in preference to showing the clubs. In general, when your hand is worth just one bid, give preference to supporting partner's major suit.

28. Opener's Rebid after a Response at the Two Level

A partner who responds at the two level will have some values. The opener's first duty is to indicate whether his own hand is better than minimum.

After, say, one heart—two clubs, two hearts is a limited rebid. Two diamonds is consistent with a minimum opening, though it may also be the bid on quite a strong hand. In general, you expect responder to bid again over any change of suit: since he has bid at the two level he should either have all-round values or be able to rebid his suit.

A rebid of two notrump, in a sequence such as one spade—two diamonds—two notrump, shows a hand with some "body," in the range of 15 to 17.

A new suit at the three level, one spade—two hearts—three clubs, implies a strong hand with RE-VERSING VALUES. The fit with partner's suit is an important consideration, because after the rebid of a new suit at the three level you will seldom be able to stop short of game.

Questions

You open one heart and partner responds two clubs. What do you rebid on the following hands?

1. ♠ J 5
   ♡ A Q 9 6 2
   ◊ A J 8 3
   ♣ 6 4   12

2. ♠ K Q 7 4
   ♡ A J 8 5 3
   ◊ A 6 2
   ♣ 3   14

3. ♠ A 4 3
   ♡ A K 7 6 2
   ◊ Q 10 5
   ♣ K 8   16

4. ♠ A Q 4
   ♡ K J 10 9 7 4
   ◊ J 2
   ♣ K 10   14

Answers

1. You have a minimum opening, but this does not mean that you must make the limited rebid of two hearts. Develop naturally with two diamonds.

2. You are not strong enough to reverse with two

spades, especially as you have no fit for clubs. Rebid two hearts.

3. With 16 points you are in the right range for two notrump, and this is the obvious bid.

4. The playing strength justifies a rebid of three hearts.

29. Developments after an Opening One Notrump

To go back to responses for a moment, there are many systems of responding to one notrump. The following is suggested:

• SIMPLE TAKE-OUT INTO TWO OF A SUIT (*other than two clubs*): A weak response. Opener is expected to pass. He may, occasionally, raise a major suit if he is maximum and has a good fit.

• JUMP TAKE-OUT INTO THREE OF A SUIT: Forcing to game.

• RAISES TO TWO NOTRUMP OR THREE NOTRUMP: Playing 16 to 18, raise to two notrump on 8, to three notrump on 9.

• RESPONSE OF TWO CLUBS: When you enter the wide world of bridge you will find that your partners will expect you to play the STAYMAN CONVENTION. A response of two clubs asks the opener to show a 4-card major if he has one. Lacking four cards of either major, opener bids two diamonds; with four of each he bids two hearts and may show the spades later. That is the basis and all you need to know at this point: entire books have been written on this convention!

Questions

Partner opens one notrump (16–18). What do you respond on the following hands?

1. ♠ 9 5 4 2
   ♡ 6 3
   ◇ J 5
   ♣ Q 10 8 7 4

2. ♠ A 9
   ♡ 5 4
   ◇ K 10 8 6 2
   ♣ J 9 4 3

3. ♠ 3 2
   ♡ K 10 7 4
   ◇ A 8 5 2
   ♣ 9 6 4

4. ♠ A 10 5 3 2
   ♡ 8 4
   ◇ 5 2
   ♣ K 9 5 3

Answers

1. On a weak hand containing a club suit you must pass unless you propose to bid two clubs and proceed to three clubs over an unfavorable response. Here it is better to let partner play one notrump.

2. Only 8 points, but the 5-card suit will surely produce extra tricks. Raise to three notrump.

3. Bid a Stayman two clubs, hoping to find a 4–4 fit in hearts. If partner obliges by rebidding two hearts you can raise to three; if he rebids two diamonds or two spades you transfer to two notrump.

4. This is a difficult hand to value because much will depend on the fit. With a partner who plays the same method, you can bid two clubs and follow with three spades, not forcing.

OPENING BIDS OF MORE THAN ONE

30. The Opening Bid on Very Strong Hands

On very strong hands you open with a bid at the two level. Most hands from 21 upwards come into this category and so do a few powerful hands of not more than, perhaps, 15 points. The general scheme is as follows:

Opening two diamonds, two hearts or two spades
These are forcing for one round. The weakness response is two notrump.

Opening two clubs
This is forcing to game, except in the sequence two clubs—two diamonds (weakness response)—two notrump, which suggests about 23 to 24 points in the opener's hand.

Opening two notrump
This indicates a balanced hand of about 21 to 22.

31. Opening Two Bids and Responses

Opening two bids, in this context, means opening bids of two diamonds, two hearts or two spades. (Two clubs has a special meaning.) An opening two bid should possess both power and quality. These are typical examples:

44

(a) ♠ A Q J. 10 6 2   (b) ♠ 6
      ♡ —   ♡ A K J 9 7 5
      ◇ A Q J 4 2 14 ◇ A K 10
      ♣ 5 3   ♣ K J 4 18

      (c) ♠ A 5
          ♡ 7 6
          ◇ A K Q 10 8 5
          ♣ A 10 5   17

Note that these are all powerful one-suited or two-suited hands. The two bid is not designed for hands that possess high cards but no great playing strength.

The responder must in no circumstances pass a two bid, because the opener may have game in his own hand. The weakness (or NEGATIVE) response is two notrump. Over that, a simple change of suit is forcing for one round. On hand (a) you would open two spades and bid three diamonds over two notrump; on (b) you would open two hearts and rebid three hearts, not forcing; on (c) you would open two diamonds and raise two notrump to three notrump, taking a chance on the heart suit.

There are no specific requirements for a POSITIVE response. Responder may bid a suit of his own at the two level on the equivalent of an ace and a king. He would require more substance to respond at the three level.

A single raise of partner's suit, two hearts—three hearts, is forcing and promises an ace. When this style is played, a raise to four hearts shows fair support but no ace.

Questions

Partner has opened two hearts. What do you respond on the following hands?

1. ♠ A 10 7 4   2. ♠ 8 3
   ♡ 8 5 3   ♡ 7 4   *9*
   ◊ J 6 4 2 *5*   ◊ K Q 9 7 2
   ♣ 9 5   ♣ K J 10 5

3. ♠ 5 4   4. ♠ 5
   ♡ J 2   ♡ 10 8 7 3
   ◊ J 9 7 5 3 *9*   *2* ◊ Q 9 5 2 *2*
   ♣ A K 6 2   ♣ 10 6 4 2

Answers

1. Raise to three hearts. You have an ace (as required for a direct raise) and opposite an opening two bid x x x or Q x is adequate trump support.

2. Worth a positive of three diamonds, because the suit may bring in as many as five tricks if partner holds the ace.

3. Three clubs is preferable to three diamonds. Partner wants to know where your sure tricks are.

4. Lacking an ace, you cannot give a single raise, and a double raise would overstate your values. For the moment, you must give the negative response of two notrump.

32. Opening Two Clubs and Responses

An opening bid of two clubs is a CONVENTION (not connected with clubs) and is forcing to game except when the opener rebids two notrump over the weakness response of two diamonds.

Unlike a two bid, two clubs will not necessarily contain a powerful suit. You would open two clubs on either of the following hands:

(a)   ♠ A K 10 3   (b)   ♠ A K J 4
      ♡ A J 9 4 2   ♡ 3   22
      ◊ A 5   20   ◊ A K 7 5
      ♣ A 4   ♣ A K 10 8

Game is not *certain* in either case, but that is not the sole consideration. By opening two clubs you ensure time to develop your hand.

The sequence two clubs—two diamonds—two notrump shows a balanced 23 to 24 points in opener's hand. Responder may pass with a valueless hand.

The traditional standard for a positive response is an ace and a king, or a K Q and a king; but responder may use his judgment.

Questions

The bidding has begun two clubs—two diamonds—two spades. What would you bid now on the following hands?

1.   ♠ 6 3   3   2.   ♠ 8 3
    ♡ 5 2   ♡ Q 9 7 4   9
    ◊ Q 10 8 7 3   ◊ K 8 6 3
    ♣ J 6 5 2   ♣ K J 5

3.   ♠ Q J 4 2
    ♡ 7 3 2
    ◊ 5   4
    ♣ J 8 7 5 3

Answers

1. It is quite safe to bid three diamonds. Even if opener has no interest in the suit, it may fill a gap and enable him to bid three notrump.

2. Jump to three notrump. It will otherwise be diffi-

cult to express the modest values in the other three suits.

3. Three spades would not be a mistake, but a jump to four spades would express the hand better—good trumps, a ruffing value, and no ace. (If you held an ace you would bid three spades only, leaving the opener room to make a slam try below game level.)

33. Opening Two Notrump and Responses

The range for an opening two notrump is from a "good" 20 to 22. You could open two notrump on any of the following hands:

(a) ♠ K J 7 4   (b) ♠ A Q 4
    ♡ A Q 10 3   ♡ A J
    ◇ K 5   ◇ A K Q 10 6
    ♣ A Q J   ♣ 9 7 4

(c) ♠ A 10
    ♡ K Q J 8 5
    ◇ A Q J
    ♣ K 7 3

Responder can raise on 4 points or on less with a 5-card suit. A TAKE-OUT into three of a suit is forcing. A jump to four hearts or four spades is best played as a STOP BID, offering no prospects of a slam.

Three clubs over two notrump is Stayman, asking opener to show a 4-card major. Lacking four of a major, opener may bid three diamonds when he has four diamonds, or three notrump when his only 4-card suit is clubs. (The same style can be played after the sequence two clubs—two diamonds—two notrump.)

Questions

Partner has opened two notrump. What do you respond on the following hands?

1. ♠ 4
   ♡ 9 7 6 5 3 2
   ◇ K 9   ⌐
   ♣ 10 8 5 3

2. ♠ K 8 7 5 3
   ♡ 4 2
   ◇ 10 6 4   ⌐
   ♣ 9 6 2

3. ♠ 5 2
   ♡ K 10 8 4
   ◇ Q 9 7 4   ⌐
   ♣ 6 3 2

Answers

1. There should be a good play for four hearts and a direct game bid is the best action. To bid three hearts and follow with four hearts over three notrump would give the impression of a stronger hand.

2. With 5–3–3–2 distribution it is usually better to play for game in notrump. Prefer three notrump to three spades, which would invite a raise in the suit.

3. Bid three clubs (Stayman). If the opener can show hearts, four hearts may be a safer contract than three notrump.

34. Opening Bids of Three and Four

Opening suit bids of three and four (or five of a minor) are PRE-EMPTIVE: the aim is to buy the contract in your long suit before the opponents can get together.

As these bids are defensive and likely to be doubled, vulnerability and position at the table are important considerations. Supposing that as dealer you hold:

(a) ♠ K J 10 9 6 4 3   (b) ♠ 4
     ♡ 9 7 5   ♡ A K J 9 6 3 2
     ♢ 6 2   ♢ 8 7 5
     ♣ 4   ♣ 6 2

On (a) you could open three spades not vulnerable. On (b) you might open four hearts not vulnerable, three hearts if vulnerable.

Responder must bear in mind that the pre-emptive opener will have less in high cards than if he had opened with a bid of one, and also that he will expect to play in the suit he has named. In principle, it is wrong to fight the opener's suit, unless you are bidding a major over a minor.

Questions

With neither side vulnerable partner deals and opens three spades. What do you respond on the following hands?

1. ♠ 5
    ♡ A J 10 3
    ♢ A K 9 5 2
    ♣ K Q 4

2. ♠ 6 2
    ♡ K 10 5
    ♢ A J 8 7
    ♣ K Q 8 2

3. ♠ —
    ♡ K 5
    ♢ A Q 10 7 6
    ♣ A Q 9 8 4 3

Answers

1. Bid four spades, not three notrump. If partner were to pass three notrump, assuming that you had your reasons for making this bid, you would surely find it difficult to establish his spade suit and enter dummy to run it. Remember he has less in high cards than if he had opened with a bid of one.

2. Pass three spades and hope to make it.

3. Annoying, but don't seek to improve the contract by bidding four clubs, which would be forcing.

OTHER BIDDING SITUATIONS

35. Responding after an Original Pass

Sequences such as one heart—one spade, or one heart—two diamonds, normally forcing for one round, are not forcing when the responder has passed originally. Responder should therefore avoid making tentative or exploratory bids, especially at the two level, in a suit where he has no wish to play.

A jump in a new suit by a player who has passed implies a fit for the opener's suit. This is logical because, if you could not open the bidding and had no fit for partner, you could hardly issue a strong invitation to game by jumping in a new suit.

Although the opener is *allowed* to pass a simple change of suit by a passed hand, he should not be keen to do so. If his opening was sound he should make his normal rebid.

Questions

1. You pass as dealer and your partner opens one heart in third position. What is your response on the following hands?

(a)   ♠ K 8 3
          ♡ J 4
          ◊ Q 7 6 2
          ♣ A 7 4 3

(b)   ♠ A J 8 5 3
          ♡ 5 2
          ◊ A J 7 4
          ♣ 6 3

2. Suppose that your partner had opened not one heart, but one spade. Then how would you respond on hands (a) and (b)?

Answers

1. (a) You don't want to languish in two clubs, with perhaps Q x opposite. As between on notrump, a slight UNDERBID, and two notrump, an OVERBID, prefer one notrump.

(b) Bid one spade simply—not two spades "to show a strong pass." You will miss nothing if partner cannot bid over one spade.

2. (a) Now the choice is between two spades and three spades. Prefer two spades.

(b) Jump to three diamonds. This means that you are worth at least three spades and have values in diamonds as well.

36. Bidding with a Part Score

When you have a part score of 40 or more, open aggressively and when possible choose a high-ranking bid such as one spade or one notrump, which is more difficult to overcall than one of a minor suit. At 60 on score, in particular, it is wise to set aside the strong notrump and open one notrump on anything from 14 to 18.

Adopt the same aggressive tactics when both sides have a part score. It is less risky to open with a weak hand than to intervene after opponents have opened the bidding.

When only the other side has a part score, not much is gained by a light opening of one club or one diamond, but if you can open one spade you may steal the contract.

Never "bid to the score." At 40 on score an opening two bid is strong, though not completely forcing. Opening three bids are still pre-emptive in principle, though the upper limit is extended.

Questions

Your side is 40 on score and your partner opens one heart. What do you respond on the following hands?

1. ♠ J 7 5
    ♡ 10 3
    ◊ K 8 6 4 2
    ♣ 7 6 4

2. ♠ J 4
    ♡ K 10 7 3
    ◊ A 8 5 3
    ♣ K J 9

3. ♠ K Q J 9 5 3
    ♡ 4 3
    ◊ J 10 7 2
    ♣ 3

Answers

1. You would pass if you had nothing below the line, but with 40 on score you can risk one notrump.

This response, especially over a major suit, should not be treated as forcing.

2. Raise to three hearts, although this is "one over score." If you do not express your hand naturally, you will miss easy slams.

3. You might like to bid two spades, to silence the opposition, but that would be on unconditional force. Bid one spade simply.

37. Bidding over Intervention

When an opening bid is OVERCALLED by the second player, responder should pass a moderate balanced hand, as the opener will have another opportunity. A FREE BID of one notrump over intervention suggests about 8 to 10, with a guard in opponent's suit.

It is seldom wise to double an intervening bid at the one level, but many opportunities for penalty doubles occur at the two level. A double of two hearts or any higher part score must, for safety, contain trump tricks, because if the contract is made the opponents will score game. A double of two of a minor is a less serious affair and may sometimes be made with no more than K x x in the trump suit.

When either player (opener or responder) wants to insure that the bidding will continue to game, he may signify this by bidding the opponent's suit. Such a bid does not necessarily promise first-round control (ace or void).

Questions

Your partner opens one heart and the next player overcalls with two clubs. What action do you take on the following hands?

1. ♠ K 9 7 4 2   2. ♠ K 8 6 3
   ♡ 6   ♡ Q 10 8
   ◊ J 8 5 3   ◊ 6 2
   ♣ A 8 4   ♣ A 9 7 4

3. ♠ J 7 4 2
   ♡ A 6
   ◊ K Q J 8
   ♣ A 6 3

Answers

1. This is quite a good moment for a penalty double. You will be the opening leader and have a good lead—the singleton heart. The misfit in partner's suit is itself a recommendation. Two spades would be a mistake: you are under strength for a free bid at the two level, especially as your suit is of higher rank than partner's.

2. You might well be able to defeat two clubs, but it is almost never right to double opponents at a low level when you have support for partner's suit which you have not declared. Raise to two hearts.

3. You are strong enough to bid the enemy suit, three clubs, but it is better to develop naturally with two diamonds. If the hearts and diamonds were reversed, three clubs would be correct.

38. Bidding to Game and Slam

After the first two rounds the bidding can take so many turns that it is not practical, in an introductory book like this, to begin to trace them. However, there are a few guidelines which may help you to judge whether game or slam is on the horizon.

Is game likely?

As a rule, an opening bid facing an opening bid will produce a sound play for game. Sometimes you can make small adjustments.

(a) ♠ 7 4 2　　　　　(b) ♠ 6
　　 ♡ K J 3　　　　　　　 ♡ A K 4
　　 ♢ A Q 7 6 4　　　　　 ♢ K 8 7 5 2
　　 ♣ 5 2　　　　　　　　 ♣ Q 6 5 2

In each case partner opens one spade, you respond two diamonds, and he rebids two spades. On hand (a) you have not quite the values for an opening bid, but you have trump support for a rebid suit and a doubleton. You are well worth three spades. On (b) you just have the values for an opening bid, but the lack of any fit for spades is a disadvantage; two notrump is enough.

Is Slam likely?

Slam bidding is difficult, and even experts, who have long experience and employ complicated methods, do not achieve a high proportion of success. The sensible course is to bid the easy ones and let the rest go. Here are three tests that will help on occasions to tell you whether you are in the slam zone:

• A jump rebid facing an opening bid should add up to a slam. Suppose the bidding begins one diamond— one spade—three diamonds. If as responder you have the values for an opening bid and some fit for diamonds you may expect a slam.

• If you could take an ace away from your hand and still be confident of game, it should be safe to issue a slam invitation.

• A combined count of 33 will normally afford a play for six notrump even when there is no long suit.

Cue bids and Blackwood

It is one thing to judge that a slam may be possible, another to find the best approach. Two popular methods are illustrated in this example, where as West you hold:

♠ K J 7 6 4 2	The bidding begins:	*West*	*East*
♡ 4		—	1 ♡
◇ J 3		1 ♠	3 ♠
♣ A Q 7 4		?	

A slam is likely and at this point you bid four clubs. The new suit at the four level, after the trump suit has been agreed, is a CUE BID, indicating a control, usually an outside ace or void. Say that over four clubs partner bids four diamonds, showing a control in this suit. Then you bid four notrump, the BLACKWOOD CONVENTION, asking partner how many aces he holds. He responds as follows: with no ace or four aces, five clubs; with one ace, five diamonds; with two aces, five hearts; with three aces, five spades.

Most players use Blackwood far too often. Most slams depend on a variety of factors, not just aces. The time for Blackwood is when you can say to yourself, "So long as we are not missing two aces, a small slam is safe."

39. Review of Constructive Bidding

We have looked at all basic situations in constructive bidding, except for action by responder after a take-out double, which is described in Section 47. In this summary it is necessary to quote "points" as a form of shorthand; but remember, once again, that in valuation many factors come into the reckoning.

Opening suit bids of one and responses

Open one of a suit on 13 to 21, also on 11 to 12 with a long suit or two good suits.

Respond one of a suit on 5 to 16. This is forcing for one round.

Respond two of a suit on 9 to 16, also on 7 to 8 with a rebiddable 6-card suit. The response is forcing for one round.

Jump in a new suit, forcing to game, with upwards of 17, or on less with a powerful suit or strong support for partner's suit.

Raise to two with 2 to 9, depending on trump support and ruffing values (i.e. short suits).

Raise to three with 10 to 15, four trumps and ruffing values. The response is forcing.

Raise to four on about 4 to 10 with strong distributional support. The response is pre-emptive.

The opener's first rebid

After a suit response at the level of one, bid one notrump on 13 to 15, two notrump on 17 to 19. A new suit at the two level, if of higher rank than opener's first suit (e.g. 1 diamond—1 spade—2 hearts) is a "reverse," showing good values.

After a response of one notrump raise to two notrump on 17 to 18, to three notrump on 19.

After a suit response at the level of two, rebid two notrump on 15 to 17, three notrump on 18 to 20. A reverse (e.g. 1 heart—2 diamonds—2 spades) shows additional values.

Notrump bids and responses

Open one notrump on 16 to 18. Raise to two notrump on 8. A take-out into two of a suit is weak. A take-out into two clubs is Stayman, asking opener to name a 4-card major or to bid two diamonds.

Open two notrump on 21 to 22. In response, three clubs is Stayman, asking opener to name a 4-card major, or to bid three diamonds with four diamonds, or three notrump when his only 4-card suit is clubs.

Opening suit bids of three and four

Open with a bid of three, in first or second hand, with a long suit and about 4 to 8 points. Open with a bid of four on a long suit and about 5 to 10 points. In third or fourth hand the range for both openings is wider.

Opening two bids

Open two spades, two hearts or two diamonds on a powerful hand with a range of about 15 to 21, forcing for one round.

Opening two clubs

Open two clubs on game-going hands from about 19 upwards. The opening is forcing to game except in the sequence two clubs—two diamonds (weakness response)—two notrump.

Part III

DEFENSIVE AND COMPETITIVE BIDDING

We have been concerned up to now with constructive bidding by the opener and his partner. On many hands, of course, the defenders will enter the bidding. Sometimes this side will have the balance of the cards and obtain the final contract without a struggle. At other times the strength will be about equally divided and the two sides will compete to win the contract in the denomination that suits them best.

40. Simple Overcalls at the Level of One

The defending side, for the most part, has different objectives, and a different strategy, from the side that opens the bidding. Quite often the main purpose of overcalling is to harass the opposition. Suppose that the opponent on your right opens one club and, not vulnerable, you hold:

♠ K J 9 7 4 3
♡ 8 2
◇ Q 10 6 3
♣ 5

Not a great hand, to be sure, but by overcalling with one spade you may achieve one or more of the following aims:

• By bidding the suit you may deflect the opponents from reaching three notrump.

• Whatever the final contract, you will have indicated a good line of attack to your partner.

• Your bid may lead to a profitable sacrifice of four spades over an opponent's four hearts or three notrump.

• A more subtle point: by overcalling one club with one spade you occupy BIDDING SPACE, making it more difficult for the opening side to develop the auction. In particular, you prevent the responder from bidding hearts at the one level.

Points are not important, but the normal range for an overcall at the one level is from about 5 to 13 not vulnerable, 7 to 14 vulnerable. The suit should be respectable, especially when vulnerable.

Questions

The opponent on your right opens one diamonds. What would you call on the following hands (a) with neither side vulnerable, (b) with both sides vulnerable?

1. ♠ 6 3 2
    ♡ A Q 8 4
    ◇ 5 2
    ♣ K 7 5 2

2. ♠ A J 8 2
    ♡ 6 4 2
    ◇ K 10 8 3
    ♣ 5 4

3. ♠ Q 10 9 7 5 4
    ♡ A 8
    ◇ 6 4
    ♣ 8 5 2

Answers

1. (a) It is better to pass because the hand is short of playing tricks (should partner support you) and the overcall does not take away any bidding space. (b) To make a vulnerable overcall would be very unsound.

2. (a) There is an added reason now for passing rather than making a weak overcall: you are strong defensively and should be willing to give the opponents a little rope. (b) Now these arguments apply with greater force.

3. (a) It is fair to overcall with one spade, not vulnerable. (b) Vulnerable, you are too short of tricks—pass.

41. Simple Overcalls at the Level of Two

At the two level you are much more exposed to a penalty double, and before overcalling at this level you must be reasonably confident that if you encounter a weak hand opposite (your partner's) you will not be SET (or go down) more than three tricks. A suit of Q J 10 8 x x offers much better assurance of four tricks in the play than A K x x x.

It is, nevertheless, correct to take a reasonable chance when you have well defined objectives—for example, to show a lead to your partner or to discourage opponents from bidding three notrump.

It is rare to overcall on a 4-card suit. Vulnerable, an overcall at the two level always proclaims a good suit, which can be supported on Q x or x x x in partner's hand.

Questions

The opponent on your right opens one heart. What would you call on the following hands (a) with neither side vulnerable, (b) with both sides vulnerable?

1. ♠ 6 4
    ♡ A 8
    ◇ K Q 10 8 5
    ♣ 9 7 6 3

2. ♠ J 7 3
    ♡ K 10 2
    ◇ Q 4
    ♣ A Q 8 6 4

3. ♠ 4
    ♡ 7 4
    ◇ K J 8 6 5 2
    ♣ A 10 7 3

Answers

1. (a) You might catch a cold in two diamonds doubled and certainly it would not be wrong to pass; but by overcalling you prevent a response of one spade or one notrump and you suggest a good line of defense. (b) Vulnerable, the risk of an 800 penalty (down 3 doubled) is too great, and in any case partner will expect more.

2. (a) Now your only 5-card suit is weak and the hand is defensive in character: a bad overcall. (b) Vulnerable, you could lose 800 while saving nothing—pass.

3. (a) A moderate hand, but if you lose 300 in two diamonds doubled you will surely be saving a game. An important consideration is that your overcall will deflect partner from leading a spade against an eventual notrump contract. (b) Vulnerable, the hand is too weak—pass.

42. Overcalling with One Notrump

An overcall of one notrump is more exposed to the elements than any other call at a low level. The partner of the opening bidder with 9 or 10 points can easily judge that his side has the balance of the cards (adding these points to his partner's likely 13 or so) and will be quick to double. If the overcaller has no escape suit he will be trapped on the ropes.

On a balanced hand it is imprudent to overcall with less than 15 not vulnerable, and even then much will depend on the nature of your GUARD in the opponent's suit. It is far better to hold, say, Q 10 x x than A x x.

Questions

The opponent on your right opens one heart. With neither side vulnerable, what action do you take on the following hands?

1. ♠ A 8
   ♡ K 8 7
   ◊ J 5 3
   ♣ A K 10 9 4

2. ♠ K J
   ♡ A 7 4 2
   ◊ A 8 2
   ♣ Q 6 4 3

3. ♠ Q 8 2
   ♡ A J 10 4
   ◊ K J 6 2
   ♣ Q 3

Answers

1. This is a fair hand for an overcall of one no-trump. If doubled, you can consider running to two clubs. An immediate overcall of two clubs would not reflect the high-card strength.

2. Here, to overcall with one notrump would be both dangerous and pointless. Your 14 points will not even pull their normal weight: you have only one stop in the enemy suit and the doubleton K J of spades is a poor holding.

3. Now you have a good holding in hearts and it is unlikely that one notrump doubled would be expensive. However, it is tactically better to pass, lying in wait. This is called a TRAP PASS and would be still more effective against vulnerable opponents.

43. Jump Overcalls

Two hearts over an opening one diamond, or three clubs over one spade, is a JUMP OVERCALL.

It is usual to play weak jump overcalls. Not vulnerable, you would bid two spades over a suit opening on any of these hands:

(a) ♠ K J 10 7 5 3
♥ 10 8 6
♦ 9 7 4
♣ 3

(b) ♠ Q J 9 8 7 5 2
♥ 4
♦ 3 2
♣ 7 5 4

(c) ♠ A Q 10 6 5 3
♥ 6 5
♦ Q 7 4
♣ 8 2

Hand (c) would be close to maximum for this type of call.

44. Doubling for Take-out

One convention in bidding is so familiar that players do not think of it as a convention at all. This is the so-called TAKE-OUT DOUBLE. The commonest example occurs when the bidding has been opened on your right and you have a useful hand on which you want to launch a counter-attack. South opens one diamond and you as West hold:

♠ K J 8 5
♡ A 9 6 4 2
♢ 4
♣ K Q 8

You could overcall in hearts but might miss a much better fit in spades. You double, saying to partner, "My hand is quite good. Tell me where your strength lies."

It is naturally very important to distinguish between a take-out double and a penalty double. The following definition holds good for most situations:

If partner has already made a bid of any kind, then a double is a penalty double made with the expectation of beating the contract.

If partner has not made any positive call, a double of one or two of a suit is for take-out if made at the first opportunity of doubling this suit.

In the following sequences (T) stands for take-out,
(P) for penalty.

	South	West	North	East
1.	1♠	dble (T)	2♣	dble(P)
2.	1♡	pass	1♠	pass
	2♡	dble (P)		
3.	1♢	dble (T)	3♢	pass
	pass	dble (T)		

In the third sequence West is doubling at the three
level. A double at this level is normally for penalties,
but here West has doubled one diamond, so he must be
prepared for any suit partner may bid.

45. The Requirements for a
Take-out Double

The requirements for a take-out double vary according to circumstances, such as vulnerability, position at the table, whether you have passed previously,
and so forth. Returning to the situation when South
has opened, the requirements for a take-out double by
West are:

• The values for an opening bid; but to some extent
good distribution will compensate for relative lack of
high cards. With, say, ♠ K J 8 5 ♡ A 9 6 4 2 ♢ 4
♣ Q 10 8, which is a king weaker than the example in
No. 44, West can double one diamond because of the
excellent support for both majors.

• Essentially, the player who doubles must be able
to deal with any response that partner may make. This
means that, unless you have a good suit of your own,

68

you must not double when you are weak in a suit which partner may well bid in response.

Overcalling in the opponent's suit

With an exceptionally strong hand, particularly a two-suiter, you may overcall in the opponent's suit, bidding two diamonds over one diamond. This is forcing for at least two rounds and so gives you time to give a picture of your distribution.

Questions

The opponent on your right opens one heart. What action do you take on the following hands?

1. ♠ K 7 4   2. ♠ Q 10 7 4
    ♡ 5   ♡ 3
    ◇ A K 9 6 3   ◇ A 9 6 3 2
    ♣ A J 8 4   ♣ K 7 4

    3. ♠ A K 10 8 6
        ♡ —
        ◇ A K J 7 4 2
        ♣ K 9

Answers

1. The support for spades is moderate, but the hand qualifies for a take-out double.

2. The distribution is good (5–4–3–1 is appreciably better for offensive purposes than 4–4–4–1), but the hand is too weak in high cards for a double. It would be a sound double if you had passed originally and so limited your hand.

3. With this strong two-suiter an overcall in the opponent's suit is the best move. Bid two hearts.

46. Responding to a Take-out Double

These are the general lines of action to be followed when your partner has made a take-out double:

• If the third player (opener's partner) has made any call other than a pass, you as fourth player may pass on a bad hand.

• Assuming that third hand has passed, you as doubler's partner with a weak or moderate hand should make a minimum response in your best suit. If your main strength is in the opponent's suit, you may bid one notrump.

• With a fair hand, about 8 to 10 points, or less with a long suit, make a jump response. This is not forcing.

• To show a likely game hand, opposite a double, bid the opponent's suit. With a strong suit of your own you may go straight to game.

• With exceptional strength in the opponent's suit, not less than Q J 10 9 x, you may make a PENALTY PASS, converting the take-out double into a penalty double. (Then any further doubles by your side will be penalty doubles.)

Questions

South opens one diamond, West doubles and North passes. What action should you as East take on the following hands?

1. ♠ 7 6 4
   ♡ J 5 2
   ◇ 9 7 2
   ♣ 10 6 5 2

2. ♠ 8 4 3 2
   ♡ 7 4
   ◇ K J 9 7 3
   ♣ Q 6

3. ♠ K 9 4 3   4. ♠ J 8 7 3
   ♥ A 5   ♥ A 10 8 5
   ♦ 8 4 2   ♦ 4 3
   ♣ K 10 6 4   ♣ K 10 7

Answers

1. The one thing you must not do is pass, allowing South to play in one diamond doubled and make overtricks. Nor is it clever to bid one heart "to keep it low." Bid dutifully two clubs, and if disaster follows it will not be your fault.

2. The diamonds are not solid enough for a penalty pass. The choice is between one spade and one notrump. Prefer one spade.

3. Not a great hand, but you must distinguish between fair hands and poor ones. Respond two spades. This is not forcing.

4. Respond two diamonds, asking partner in turn to bid *his* best suit. If he bids two hearts or two spades, as is likely, you will raise to three.

47. Action by Third Hand over a Take-out Double

When your partner's opening bid has been doubled by the second player, you act as follows:

• With moderate values, you pass.

• With a moderate hand but a fair suit, you bid the suit at minimum level. This is not forcing, or even encouraging.

• With a balanced hand of about 7 to 9 you bid one notrump.

• With moderate values but support for partner's suit, raise to the limit—and beyond! Partner will recognize that you are bidding defensively.

• With support for partner and upwards of 9 points (so that you do not need to pre-empt), or with a fair all-round hand but no support, redouble. This tells partner that you have the situation in hand, one way or another, and will bid again if he passes.

Questions

South opens one heart and West doubles. What action should you, North, take on the following hands?

1. ♠ 5
   ♡ K 7 6 4
   ◇ Q 10 8 6 3
   ♣ 9 5 2

2. ♠ Q 10 8 7
   ♡ 5 4
   ◇ A 9 6 3
   ♣ K J 4

3. ♠ 8 6 4
   ♡ 5
   ◇ Q 7 2
   ♣ K J 9 6 4 3

Answers

1. Raise to three hearts, attempting to shut out the next player. This is in no sense an invitation to game.

2. A typical hand for a redouble. If opponents are vulnerable you will probably play for penalties—that is to say, you or your partner will double whatever they call.

3. Had there been no intervention it would have been unsound to respond at the level of two. As it is, you can bid two clubs. The failure to redouble limits your hand.

48. Bidding in the Protective [or Balancing] Position

When an opening bid is followed by two passes, the fourth player may PROTECT on less than would be considered necessary for an immediate overcall. He should not think, "I will pass before worse befalls," but "My partner has probably passed on quite a good hand." One notrump in the protective position suggests only 11 to 14 points, and a guard in the opponent's suit is not essential. One of a suit is limited; with upwards of 13, prefer to double.

Whenever the opponents drop the bidding at a low level, it is reasonable to assume that they are limited and that partner, even though he may not have spoken, . must have some values. It is highly important to judge when to BALANCE, so that your side will not be outbid in the part-score area.

Questions

The bidding begins:

South	West	North	East
1 ♡	pass	2 ♡	pass
pass	?		

Now West is in the protective, or balancing, position. What action should he take on the following hands?

1. ♠ A J 7 4   2. ♠ J 10 7
  ♥ 5 4 3   ♥ 4 2
  ♦ A 10 5 2   ♦ A J 3 2
  ♣ Q 4   ♣ A 10 7 4

3. ♠ 4 2
 ♥ 9 5
 ♦ A Q 10 5
 ♣ K J 8 5 3

Answers

1. This would be a poor overcall of one spade, but after opponents have subsided in two hearts it is right to compete with two spades. Generally speaking, you should be reluctant to let opponents buy the contract at a low level when they have found a fit.

2. Now you can balance with a take-out double. It is true that this is not a double of hearts "at the first opportunity," but it is much more useful to play the double for take-out than for penalties.

3. One would not expect a beginner to find this answer, but the clever bid (with a tolerably clever partner) is two notrump! This cannot be genuine since you did not bid over one heart, and since you have by-passed two spades your interest must lie in the minor suits. The UNUSUAL NOTRUMP indicates length in the two lowest unbid suits.

49. Other Doubling and Redoubling Situations

Double by the opening bidder

The player who has opened the bidding will often make a take-out double to show reserves of strength. The bidding goes:

South	West	North	East
1◇	1♠	pass	2♠
dble			

South is saying, "I am not prepared to let them play in two spades. Bid something!" He will hold a hand of this type:

♠ x
♡ A J x x
◇ A K x x x
♣ A Q 10

Double of one notrump

A double of an opponent's one notrump opening is by definition for penalties rather than for take-out. Partner should pass on a weak balanced hand, but may rescue on a weak hand containing a 5-card suit.

It is virtually never right to double a strong notrump of 16–18. You will find that some opponents will play a weak notrump of 12–14. Still be wary of doubling on less than 16 or so, because there will be no escape from a heavy penalty if the opener's partner holds the balance of the cards.

Defense against opening pre-emptive bids

The best defense to employ against an opponent's opening three bid is one of the most debatable subjects in the game. Most players employ what are called OP-TIONAL DOUBLES. In effect, the double is much more for take-out than for penalties. There are numerous other conventional systems, all of which work well on occasions.

SOS redouble

In certain part-score situations a redouble is bid for rescue purposes. Say that the bidding goes:

South	West	North	East
1 ♡	1 ♠	dble	pass
pass	redble		

If West were happy with one spade doubled he would pass. He is saying here, "My spades are not robust. We had better try something else." (In more advanced circles a redouble by *East* in this sequence would also be SOS, meaning "I hate your bid!")

50. The Mathematics of Sacrifice Bidding

The scoring at rubber bridge is deceptive because no entry is made above the line for the first game made by either side. This game nevertheless has an "equity value" of between 300 and 350, apart from the trick score. It pays to SACRIFICE and go down 300 to save a game at any time, and to go down 500 to save the rubber game (which is worth precisely the 620 or so which is entered on the scoresheet).

Part scores also have an equity value, more difficult to assess. To lose 300 to save a part score is not a calamity. It pays to be venturesome in this area because quite often the opponents will misjudge and bid too high themselves. Then you will obtain a small penalty instead of conceding a part score.

51. Review of Defensive Bidding

Point-count standards are mentioned in some cases in the following summary, but playing tricks, derived from good suits and strong distribution, are more important than high cards.

Suit overcalls at the level of one

Not vulnerable, the overcall may be little more than a nuisance bid on a long suit. Vulnerable, the overcall must have more substance; range, about 7 to 14.

Suit overcalls at the level of two

The range is about 7 to 14 and a fair suit is essential, especially when vulnerable.

Overcall of one notrump

The standard on a balanced hand is about 15 to 17 not vulnerable, 16 to 18 vulnerable.

Jump overcalls

Usually played as weak—a good suit but not more than 8 or 9 points.

Take-out double

Correct on most hands of 14 upwards and on less with good preparedness for all suits.

Responding to a take-out double

Assuming that third hand has passed, on a weak hand bid your best suit at minimum level, or one notrump when the main strength is the opponent's suit; jump on fair values, about 8 to 10; when stronger, either bid a direct game or bid the opponent's suit; pass only with exceptional strength in the opponent's suit.

Protecting in fourth hand

When an opening bid is followed by two passes, protect on less than would be expected from an immediate overcall; bid one notrump on 11 to 14; on good hands, begin with a take-out double.

Part IV
TRICKS IN A SINGLE SUIT

The first stage in play is to know how to count the cards and remember what has been played in each suit. Equally important is knowing how to handle combinations in a single suit.

Eventually, counting each suit to 13 will become so automatic you will do it without thinking, just as a typist can type without looking at the keys. You will instinctively have a feeling for the distribution of a suit, knowing how many cards are left after one or two rounds.

Before you can form a plan, you need to know how many tricks various holdings are likely to produce. Aside from top winners, tricks are developed by forcing out high cards held by your opponents, by establishing long cards (that is, low cards that gain in rank after the high cards have been played), and by taking advantage of the positional factor in play (finessing).

52. Winning Tricks by Promotion

Apart from laying down aces and kings, the simplest way to promote tricks when you are declarer is to force out high cards held by the opponents.

	DUMMY		DUMMY
(a)	K J 10	(b)	Q J 9 6 3
	Q 6 4		10 5
	DECLARER		DECLARER

With (a) you force out the ace and establish two sure tricks. With (b) you have to force out both the ace and king; when you have done this you have set up three winners.

In many cases the number of tricks that can be promoted will depend on the position of the adverse cards.

(c)	K 5	(d)	K Q 5
	7 4 2		6 4 3

To have any chance of developing a trick with (c), you must lead towards the K x. If the ace is on your left, "under" the king, you will make a trick, but not if the ace is held by East. With (d) you hope to make two tricks. You begin by leading low towards the honors; if the king is not overtaken by the ace you return to your hand to lead again towards the Q x, making two tricks whenever West holds the ace.

Note that it is essential in both cases to lead up to the high cards, not away from them. This principle has a very wide application. Here is one more example:

(e)   Q J 4

A 10 5   K 8 7 3

                9 6 2

You can make a trick with North's Q J x, but only by leading each time from your hand.

80

53. Establishing Long Cards

The other standard way of developing extra tricks is by establishing low cards as winners, Approximately five tricks out of thirteen on an average deal played in notrump are won by low cards, which at the beginning of the play had no obvious value. Quite often, low-card winners can be established without losing the lead:

(a)   K 7 4 2   (b)   K 7 4 2

A Q 5   A Q 8 5

With (a) you hold 7 cards in the two hands (yours and dummy's), including the three top honors. If the suit is divided 3–3 against you, dummy's fourth card will be a winner. You play off ace, queen and king; if everybody has followed suit you know that the last card, the thirteenth, is good. This would be a comparatively lucky division, for the odds are against a 3–3 break of six outstanding cards. With (b), where you have 8 of a suit, you have much better prospects of establishing the fourth round, for a 3–2 break in opponents' hands is much more likely than 4–1.

In many cases you will need to surrender one or more tricks when on the way to establishing long cards.

(c) A Q 6 4 2   (d) A K 8 6 4 2

K 5   7 5

With (c) you may be lucky, finding a 3–3 break. More likely, the suit will break 4–2, and to establish the fifth round you will need to surrender the fourth.

With (d) you are bound to lose at least one trick, but if the suit breaks 3–2 you will make five tricks in the end.

In the next two examples you combine the two techniques of promoting high cards and establishing low ones.

(e)   7 4 2

J 10 8   A 9

    K Q 6 5 3

(f) K 9 7 6 5 2

A 4   Q 10

    J 8 3

In (e) you begin by leading low towards the honor combination. A defender will normally play low from A 9 in second hand, so the king wins. You cross to dummy for the next lead and now the ace appears. On the third round the jack falls under the queen. You make four tricks with this holding whenever A x or A x x is under the K Q. In (f), again, the cards lie well. You play low toward the king; when this holds you play a second round, on which the ace and queen fall together.

The principle of leading towards high cards may apply even when you hold a stronger combination, such as Q J 10 x x or K Q J x. These are two aspects of the same problem:

(g) Q J 10 7 4

K   A 9 6 2

    8 5 3

(h)   K Q J 5

A 8   10 9 6 3

    7 4 2

With (g) it would cost a trick if you made the first lead from dummy. The queen would lose to West's king, and East's A 9 6 would be worth two more tricks to the defense. With (h) you must aim to lead twice from your hand. If you lead low to the king and then lead the queen, you make only two tricks instead of three.

With this frequent combination you play to establish just one long card:

(i)   A K 7 4 2

        Q 10 8   J 9 6 3

                    5

Here you are missing seven cards, but 4–3 is by far the most likely division and after losing two tricks you may be able to establish the fifth card as a winner. (You are more likely to develop this suit in a trump contract than at notrump).

54. Simple Finesses

Every bridge player can recognize a FINESSE when he sees one, although the term is not easy to define. A finesse is an attempt by the declarer to win or promote a trick with a card that is not the highest held by his side. These are examples of a finesse against the king:

(a) ·   A Q   (b)   A 8 2

    K 4   8 3   K 7 4   9 6 5

        7 6   Q J 10 3

In (a) South leads the 6; when West plays low he finesses by playing the queen, thus making both tricks. In (b) he leads the queen and lets it run if West plays low. He follows with the jack, which West will probably cover. With the finesse right, and the suit breaking 3–3, declarer makes all four tricks.

These are examples of a finesse for the queen:

(c)	A J 7 4 2	(d)	K 7 6 4
Q 8 5	10 9 3	Q 3 2	A 5
	K 6		J 10 9 8

In (c) South lays down the king, then finesses the jack on the next lead, and makes all five tricks when the suit breaks 3–3. On (d) he leads the jack and West plays low; a low card from dummy forces the ace. South takes a second finesse when he is next on lead.

Finesses against the jack and 10 are equally common:

(e)	Q 10 5 3	(f)	J 9 6 2
J 7 4	A 9 2	A 10 4	K 8 3
	K 8 6		Q 7 5

The first play with (e), if ENTRIES allow, should be low from dummy. The king wins and declarer finesses the 10 on the way back, making three tricks altogether. With (f) a finesse of the 9 forces the king and South can make two tricks eventually.

In general, it is right to lead a *low* card when intending to finesse. The reason is seen in the heart situation on the following deal:

```
                    ♠ K 8 4
                    ♡ A Q J 5
                    ◇ K 10 2
                    ♣ K 9 7
  ♠ Q 9 6 5                          ♠ 10 7 2
  ♡ K 3              N               ♡ 9 8 6 2
  ◇ 9 8 7 4      W       E           ◇ Q J 5
  ♣ 8 6 2            S               ♣ 10 5 3
                    ♠ A J 3
                    ♡ 10 7 4
                    ◇ A 6 3
                    ♣ A Q J 4
```

South opens one notrump and North, with 16 points himself, is unlikely to stay short of six notrump. West leads the 9 of diamonds.

As neither player has much to spare, the small slam contract is borderline. North and East play low on the first trick and South wins with the ace. He will surely need to play hearts sooner or later and it is natural to tackle this suit early. Following the principle described above, he leads low to the jack, which holds. He returns to his hand with a club and again leads a low heart from his hand. When the king appears he can see twelve tricks and may eventually finesse the jack of spades for an overtrick.

You see that it would have been a mistake to lead the 10 of hearts on either the first or second round? West covers the 10 with the king and East's 9 controls the fourth round.

Here are two more examples of the importance of leading low when about to finesse:

(a)   K 10 6 2 | (b)   A K J 5

Q 8   A 9 5 | Q   9 7 6 2

    J 7 4 3 | 10 8 4 3

In each case the lead of an honor card by South would cast a trick.

55. Double and Combination Finesses

When you play for two cards to be favorably placed you are said to take a "double finesse." These are standard positions:

(a)   A Q 10   (b)   K J 9

    7 4 2   8 6 3

With (a) you begin with a finesse of the 10. This gives you a chance to make all three tricks whenever West holds both king and jack. With (b) there are two possibilities. You can play West for A Q, finessing the jack on the first round; or you can play him for Q 10, finessing the 9 on the first round.

A finesse against two cards in sequence is called a "combination finesse." This, too, is very common:

(c)   A J 10 5 | (d)   K 10 9 6

K 6 3   Q 8 4 | J 7 4   A Q 5

    9 7 2 | 8 3 2

With (c) you lead low to the 10, losing to the

queen. On the next round you finesse against the king and end up with three tricks. With (d) you lead low to the 9, which loses to the queen. On the next round you finesse the 10 (better than going up with the king) and this forces the ace.

These are other forms of combination finesse:

(e)	A J 9 5 2		(f)	K 10 8 4	
K 10 4		Q 8	Q 9 7		A J 5
	7 6 3			6 3 2	

With (e) the best chance for four tricks is to lead low and put in the 9. This forces the queen and you finesse the jack on the next round. With (f) you lead low to the 8, in effect playing West for Q 9 x or J 9 x. As the cards lie in the diagram, the 8 forces the jack and a finesse of the 10 on the next round establishes two tricks.

56. When a Finesse Is Not the Best Play

There are innumerable positions where an honor card is missing but a finesse, in the true sense, is not playable.

(a)	J 5	(b)	A 5 4
	A K 6 2		Q 8 6 3

Suppose that in (a) you lead the jack from dummy. If East holds the queen he will probably cover, so you can hardly gain. The best chance for three tricks is to lead low from hand, making three tricks whenever

West holds the queen. With (b) you might possibly steal a trick by leading the queen from hand, as a defender with K x x would probably not cover; but the normal play is low to the queen, which gains whenever East holds the king.

Quite often, too, a finesse may be playable but not represent the best chance for the maximum number of tricks.

(c)   A 5 2   (d)   A Q 5 4

           Q J 7 4   J 3

With (c) the lead of the queen may provide two *immediate* tricks, and if your aim is to make two tricks without losing the lead it will be right to finesse this way. But if the objective is to make three tricks the best play is low towards the Q J x x. This gains (as compared with leading the queen) when East holds K 10 x x or K x. Similarly, with (d), the tactical situation may demand a finesse of the queen, but if you need three tricks the best play is low from dummy; you hope to find East with K x or K x x.

A different consideration applies when you hold eight or nine cards of a suit, lacking the queen.

(e)   A 5 4   (f)   A 8 5 4

           K J 7 6 2   K J 7 6 2

In (e) you hold eight cards and the odds favor a finesse of the jack on the second round. In (f) you have nine cards and now it is mathetically better (after ace and a low one, on which East plays low) to play for the DROP of the queen; but there are often good reasons to finesse anyway.

57. Safety Plays

With many combinations a certain line of play provides, if not complete security, a well-defined extra chance.

(a)   A Q 10 6 4   (b)   K 7 5 2

       K 9 6 3   A Q 9 6 3

In (a) you have an example of a perfect SAFETY PLAY. By playing a high honor from dummy you insure five tricks for yourself even if J x x x is held by either opponent. (One opposing hand will show void, so there will be a MARKED FINESSE against the jack.) With (b), on the other hand, the first play should be the king. This enables you to pick up all the tricks when East holds J 10 x x. If West holds these cards you must lose one trick whatever you do.

The best play often depends on how many tricks you need.

(c)   9 5 4   (d)   J 7

K   J 10 8   K   10 9 8 6

  A Q 7 6 3 2   A Q 7 6 3 2

In (c) the only chance for *six* tricks is to finesse the queen, playing East for K x, but the best play for five tricks is to lay down the ace. If the king does not appear, you enter dummy in another suit for the next lead. With the combination shown in (d) you can never make six tricks and the best chance for five is to lead ace and another, gaining when West has a singleton king.

There are many situations where the safety play is to take a deep finesse.

	(e)	K 7 4		(f)	A 5
6		Q J 9 3	2		J 10 7 6 3
	A 10 8 5 2			K Q 9 8 4	

With (e) you lead the king and follow with the 7. It would normally not be good play for East to split his honors. When he plays low, the safety play is to finesse the 10. With (f) you lead the ace, followed by the 5. When East plays low, finesse the 9 if you want to be sure of four tricks.

Despite what was said earlier about the advisability of leading low when about to finesse, there are some combinations where the safety play is to begin with the high card.

	(g)	J 6 4 2		(h)	Q 7 5
—		K 10 8	J		K 9 3
	A Q 9 7 5 3			A 10 8 6 4 2	

With (g) you are intending to finesse for the king and should lead the jack from dummy. East will probably cover, and when West shows up with a void you can enter dummy for a finesse against the 10 8. Diagram (h) shows a rather special situation: if you need five tricks ace first is correct, but if you need all six tricks the only chance is to lead the queen from dummy, playing West for a singleton jack. (To drop a singleton king on either side will not help you to make six tricks.)

There are hundreds of safety, or "better chance," plays. It is excellent practice to study different combinations in this light.

Part V

THE PLAY AT NOTRUMP

Although the declarer has twenty-six cards to handle, his task is for the most part easier than that of the defenders. The tactical moves described in this chapter—suit establishment and the various forms of communication play—occur all the time and are not, as a rule, difficult to execute.

58. Counting Tricks and Forming a Plan

The first, and most important, step for the declarer is to form a plan, and the time to do this is when the dummy goes down. Before you play to the first trick, ask yourself these questions:

(1) What is the contract—in others words, how many tricks am I trying to make?

(2) How many certain winners are there?

(3) Where can I develop the extra tricks that are needed for my contract?

(4) Meanwhile, what are the dangers and how can I overcome them?

On some hands you will see at once that your contract is not in danger. But still go through your planning routine before you touch a card. Apart from the need to be careful, there is a psychological reason for this. If you play slowly when the hand is difficult, quickly when it is easy, you tell your opponents when they can relax and when they must concentrate. Also, by taking your time at trick 1, you mask your hand to some extent. For example, suppose you anticipate a particular line of attack by your opponents as soon as they obtain the lead: be prepared to meet it. The less you need to think later about the critical tricks, the less information you give away.

When it is suggested that you count "certain tricks," this does not mean that you should count only unstoppable aces and kings. If you have a suit such as A Q J x x opposite K x x you may count it as five tricks in your planning, although you might be disappointed. And a combination such K J x opposite Q 10 x x is obviously going to be worth three tricks, once you have forced out the ace. Count it as three certain tricks, provided you can be sure of time to enjoy them. What is meant by TIME in this context is explained in the next two sections.

59. Which Suit to Establish

Sometimes you will be able to make your contract by playing off aces and kings, or by running long suits, but more often you will need to develop extra tricks in at least one suit. Usually you will play your longest suit first, but not always: you have to consider the safest way to establish the tricks you need for your contract. One of the few absolutes in bridge is that you must never jeopardize your contract for the sake of possible overtricks: you stand to gain 30 or 60 and to lose 500 or so—not to mention your partner's confidence!

Playing the following hand in three notrump, you just need to count your tricks and keep your eye on the contract.

North dealer
Neither side vulnerable

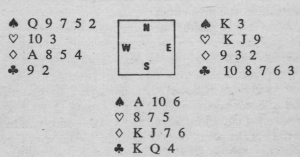

```
                    ♠ J 8 4
                    ♡ A Q 6 4 2
                    ♡ Q 10
                    ♣ A J 5

      ♠ Q 9 7 5 2                      ♠ K 3
      ♡ 10 3            N              ♡ K J 9
      ◇ A 8 5 4    W        E          ◇ 9 3 2
      ♣ 9 2            S              ♣ 10 8 7 6 3

                    ♠ A 10 6
                    ♡ 8 7 5
                    ◇ K J 7 6
                    ♣ K Q 4
```

North opens one heart and South responds with a forcing two notrump. North raises to three notrump, a game contract. South has already expressed his values (13 to 15), so does not consider any advance beyond game.

The opening lead

Most hands at notrump develop into a struggle between the two sides to establish and run their long suits. It is natural here for West to lead a spade. Certain conventions attach to the choice of card, and West would probably lead his fourth best spade, the 5.

The play

You are in three notrump, so you need to make nine tricks. When you look over the dummy you will see that your two hands contain between them three top clubs and the ace of hearts, for certain. What about the spades? With a little experience you will appreciate at once that after the suit has been led from your left you can be sure of two tricks. So six tricks are guaranteed. The hearts are capable of producing extra tricks, but the diamonds are more reliable because by simply forcing out the ace you can establish three sure winners, which is all you need for game.

You must play low from dummy at trick 1 to ensure a DOUBLE STOP in spades, where the main danger lies. East plays the king and you win with the ace. You make the next two tricks with the queen and 10 of diamonds, West declining to part with his ace. You come to your hand with a club and lead the king of diamonds, which West tops with the ace, establishing your third trick, the jack, in this suit. West may CLEAR the spades by leading queen and another, but you have the jack as a STOPPER and will have no more problems.

Sometimes the more solid and reliable suit will not produce enough tricks. Consider your prospects with the following cards:

West	East
♠ K 5	♠ A 4
♡ Q 8	♡ A 9 7 6 2
◊ Q 10 8 4 2	◊ J 9 5
♣ A Q 6 3	♣ K 8 4

You are West, playing as declarer in three notrump. North finds your soft spot with a spade lead. You are missing nine spades, and even if they are 5–4, which is the best you can hope for, there will be three spade losers after you have lost the lead twice. You have not *time* to play diamonds. You must hope to be lucky in hearts. Win the first trick with the ace of spades and lead a low heart from the table (the East hand in this case). If South has K x x you will be able to make four tricks in hearts, enough for game.

Suppose, next, that you were playing in *two* no-trump. It would then be more sensible to play for the spades to be 5–4 than to rely on the rather desperate chance in hearts. When you win the first trick, play diamonds. The opponents win and drive out your second stopper in spades. You will lose two diamonds and three spades, but that will be all.

60. Hold-up Play

South dealer, both sides vulnerable

♠ A J 7 5
♡ 6 4
◇ 8 3
♣ A J 10 7 4

♠ 9 6 2
♡ Q 9 7 5 3
◇ Q 10
♣ 8 3 2

♠ Q 10 4
♡ K J 2
◇ J 9 7 4
♣ K 9 5

♠ K 8 3
♡ A 10 8
◇ A K 6 5 2
♣ Q 6

The bidding goes:

South	West	North	East
1 ◊	pass	2 ♣	pass
2NT	pass	3NT	pass
pass	pass		

When you have reason to fear the suit that has been led, retain your control in this suit for as long as you can. The object is to exhaust one defender of the suit so that he will be unable later on to lead it back to his partner.

The opening lead

West leads the fourth best card from his longest suit, the 5 of hearts.

The play

Declarer can see six sure winners—two in spades, one in hearts, two in diamonds, and one in clubs. He therefore needs to develop three more.

There are possibilities of establishing extra tricks in both diamonds and spades, but obviously the clubs are the best prospect. Barring a 5–1 break, the suit will be worth four tricks after the king has been forced out. It may even be possible to make all five tricks (if West holds K x x).

However, the heart suit looks dangerous. When East plays the king on the first round, South must HOLD UP the ace. East returns the jack and South holds up again. He wins the third round and finesses the queen of clubs. When East takes his king he has no more hearts to play and South makes his contract easily.

It is often necessary to hold up even with a double stop in the suit led.

South dealer
Both sides
vulnerable

                    ♠ K 6 4
                    ♡ A J 5
                    ◇ Q 8 7 6 2
                    ♣ J 4

♠ J 9 8 7 3 2   ♠ Q 10
♡ Q 6 2   ♡ K 9 7
◇ K 4   ◇ A 9 5
♣ 9 6   ♣ Q 10 7 3 2

                    ♠ A 5
                    ◇ 10 8 4 3
                    ◇ J 10 3
                    ♣ A K 8 5

South opens one club, North responds one diamond, and South rebids one notrump. North raises to two notrump, inviting game, but South, having opened on a minimum, can say no more.

West leads from his long suit, the 7 of spades. South has five tricks in top cards and must aim to establish three more in diamonds. See, first, what happens if he takes the first trick with the ace of spades and leads a diamond. East will win and return the 10 of spades. West will OVERTAKE with the jack (he can count all 13 spades now) and lead a third round, forcing the king. When West wins the next diamond he will CASH his three remaining spades, giving the defense four tricks in spades and two in diamonds.

Since South is well upholstered in the other suits and

does not fear a SWITCH, he must hold off on the first round of spades and win the second. Then East will have no spade to play when he wins the first round of diamonds. South will make his contract with three tricks in diamonds and at least five winners in the other suits.

61. Ducking Play

As for an army, *communications* are everything in the play at notrump. Hold-up play, which we have just been looking at, is a way of spoiling the communications of the defending side. Ducking play is used by the declarer to maintain communications between his own hand and the dummy.

South dealer
Neither side vulnerable

```
                    ♠ A 9 7 4 2
                    ♡ Q 5
                    ◇ 8 6 2
                    ♣ 8 5 3

  ♠ J 6                              ♠ Q 10 3
  ♡ J 7 3                            ♡ K 10 8 4 2
  ◇ Q 9 7                            ◇ 10 5 3
  ♣ K J 9 6 2                        ♣ 10 7

                    ♠ K 8 5
                    ♡ A 9 6
                    ◇ A K J 4
                    ♣ A Q 4
```

South, with 21 points, opens two notrump and North raises to three notrump. His hand is balanced and he should be happy to let his partner play for 9 tricks in notrump rather than look for 10 in spades.

West leads the 6 of clubs and East plays the 10. This is not the moment for a hold-up, for to play low would expose the declarer to a lead through his A Q. He wins the first trick with the queen of clubs, cashes the king of spades, and follows with a low spade, on which West plays the jack.

It would be a bad mistake now to play the ace of spades from dummy. To insure his communications, South DUCKS, playing low from the table. East will probably overtake the jack with the queen to play a second club, returning his partner's suit. South may hold up on this trick. West wins and clears the suit for himself by leading a third club to declarer's ace.

Game is safe now. South has a third spade to play to dummy's A 9 7 and is assured of four spade tricks, one heart, two diamonds and two clubs. He runs off the spades from dummy, and if West discards a club at any point it will be safe to finesse the jack of diamonds for an overtrick. The finesse will lose, but the defense will make only four tricks.

In this last example it was essential to duck one round of spades because one trick had to be lost in any case and there was no quick side entry to the table. When declarer can afford it he will often duck for complete safety. Observe the following combinations:

(a)	A J 7 4 2		(b)	A K 8 4 3	
Q 10 8 5		3	Q 10 9 5		J
	K 9 6			7 6 2	

Assume that with (a) South needs precisely four tricks and has no side entry to the dummy. It is not safe to begin with the king, followed by a finesse of the jack: the second round must be ducked, even if West is so artful as to play the queen. With (b) declarer's objective is to make, not four tricks, but three. In this case he must duck twice, so that eventually he will make a trick with dummy's fifth card.

Ducking play is very common even when there is no anxiety about communications. Playing a suit such as A K x x opposite x x x x it is normal to duck the first round since one trick must be lost anyway. This is better than playing off ace and king and possibly setting up two winners for the defense.

It is worth noting, too, that whereas in most forms of suit establishment it is essential to lead toward high cards, ducking play is the same in effect from whichever side the lead is made.

(c)   K 8 7 5 2   (d)   A Q 7 6 4

        6 4 3   9 3

Suppose that with (c) the declarer has one side entry to the dummy, which cannot be immediately removed. To develop the long suit, he ducks the first round, and it makes no difference whether he leads from dummy or from his own hand. In (d) South can make four tricks if he can find West with K x x. On the first round he may lead low from dummy.

Part VI

THE PLAY IN A SUIT CONTRACT

The presence of a trump suit brings many new elements into play. The moves described in this Part include ruffing in the short trump hand, crossruffing dummy reversal, ruffing finesses, and ways of retaining trump control. All are typical of the play in a suit contract.

62. The Count of Losers

In a suit contract, as at notrump, it is right to form a plan before playing to the first trick, however obvious the play to the first trick may be.

The nature of the plan is different from that at notrump. These are the first two questions you put to yourself:

(1) **How many** *losers* **are there?** (This tends to be a more pertinent question than how many winners you can count.)

(2) **Shall I draw trumps? If not, why not?**

(See hand on next page.)

In this example the answer to the first question supplies the answer to the second:

South is in four spades and West leads the queen of hearts. Even if the spade finesse won't win, South has enough winners—five spades, two hearts, two diamonds and one club, after forcing out the ace of diamonds and the ace of clubs. But there are also four possible losers—one spade, one heart and two aces. Having noted this, the declarer must consider how to arrive at his winners before giving up the losers. Should he draw trumps?

```
              ♠ J 9 5
              ♡ A K 4
              ◇ K J 3
              ♣ Q 7 6 2

♠ K 3                        ♠ 8 2
♡ Q J 10 5        N          ♡ 9 7 6
◇ 10 8 5 2     W     E       ◇ A 9 6 4
♣ A 8 4           S          ♣ J 10 5 3

              ♠ A Q 10 7 6 4
              ♡ 8 3 2
              ◇ Q 7
              ♣ K 9
```

If South takes the first heart in dummy and leads the 9 of spades, letting it run, West will win and play a second heart, establishing a trick in this suit before the ace of diamonds has been forced out. The first play, therefore, should be to knock out the ace of diamonds. When the defenders play a second heart, South wins, runs diamonds, and disposes of his losing heart on the

104

third round of diamonds. Then it is safe to play trumps.

63. Ruffing in the Short Trump Hand

The commonest reason for postponing trump leads is that the declarer wants to take ruffs in the hand that is short of trumps. This is usually the dummy.

South dealer
Neither side
vulnerable

```
              ♠ K 7 4 2
              ♡ 10 6 3
              ◇ 5
              ♣ A 8 6 4 2
```

```
♠ J 10 9                      ♠ A Q 6 5 3
♡ J 7 4                       ♡ 9
◇ Q 10 8 6                    ◇ K J 9 3 2
♣ K J 5                       ♣ Q 10
```

```
              ♠ 8
              ♡ A K Q 8 5 2
              ◇ A 7 4
              ♣ 9 7 3
```

South opens one heart and West passes. Some players would respond one spade on the North hand, others would raise to two hearts. In either case the final contract will be four hearts by South.

West leads the jack of spades. West would not underlead an ace against a suit contract, so the declarer plays low from dummy. The jack holds the first trick, and when West continues with the 10 of spades, South ruffs. Assuming that trumps are not worse than 3–1, there are eight tricks "on top"—six hearts and two aces. It might be possible to develop extra tricks in clubs, but if South were to draw three rounds of trumps and then duck a club, the defense would surely attack diamonds and set up two tricks in that suit.

The safe way to establish the extra tricks is to ruff diamonds in dummy. So, after ruffing the second spade South plays the ace of diamonds, ruffs a diamond, and returns to his hand with a trump. He ruffs the third diamond in dummy. Now the best way to regain the lead is to play a third spade and ruff with the 8 of hearts. This passes off all right, because West has to follow suit in spades. South then draws the outstanding trumps and makes ten tricks by way of six hearts, two aces and two ruffs.

64. Playing a Crossruff

On some hands the declarer does not attempt to draw trumps at any point of the play. Instead, he makes as many tricks as he can in the trump suit by taking ruffs in each hand.

South dealer
Both sides vulnerable

```
                    ♠ A 8 6 4
                    ♡ 4
                    ◇ A 10 8 7
                    ♣ 10 7 5 3

  ♠ 10 7 2              N          ♠ Q J 9 3
  ♡ J 5                            ♡ K 9 6 3 2
  ◇ 6 3 2         W        E       ◇ 5
  ♣ K Q J 9 2          S           ♣ A 8 4

                    ♠ K 5
                    ♡ A Q 10 8 7
                    ◇ K Q J 9 4
                    ♣ 6
```

Bidding with fair enterprise, North-South reach six diamonds by the following route:

South	West	North	East
1 ♡	pass	1 ♠	pass
2 ◇	pass	3 ◇	pass
4 NT	pass	5 ♡	pass
6 ◇	pass	pass	pass

When North, in response to the Blackwood four no-trump, shows two aces by his five-heart bid, South judges that the small slam may require a successful heart finesse, at worst.

The play of the hand will depend to some extent on the defense. Suppose, first, that West begins with two rounds of clubs. After ruffing the second round South can see twelve almost certain tricks by way of a CROSSRUFF. He will plan to make all the trumps separately. First he should cash the ace and king of

107

spades and the ace of hearts. Then he can claim all the rest of the tricks, for nothing can prevent him from making the next eight tricks with high trumps.

Suppose, however, that West leads a trump at trick 2. South will need then to finesse the queen of hearts, cash the ace, and proceed with the crossruff as before. If the opening lead is a trump, South must be careful about the order of play: win in dummy, finesse heart queen, ruff heart; ace and king of spades, ruff heart; ruff spade, ruff last heart.

65. Reversing the Dummy

While it is usual to look for ruffs in the hand that is relatively short of trumps, sometimes it pays to take several ruffs in the longer hand. Suppose you begin with three trumps in dummy, five in your own hand: if you can ruff three times in your hand, then draw the outstanding trumps from dummy, you have extended the trick-winning power of the trump suit from five to six.

```
          ♠ A 7 5 2
          ♡ Q J 9
          ◇ K J 3
          ♣ 9 6 4

♠ K Q 10 3                      ♠ J 9 8 4
♡ 7 4 2          N              ♡ 8 6
◇ 9 7        W       E          ◇ 10 8 5 2
♣ K 10 3 2       S              ♣ J 8 7

          ♠ 6
          ♡ A K 10 5 3
          ◇ A Q 6 4
          ♣ A Q 5
```

South plays in a contract of six hearts and West leads the king of spades. The declarer has eleven top tricks. Looking at it the other way, he has two possible losers in clubs.

The simplest way to make a twelfth trick may appear to lie in a club finesse. A much stronger line is to take three spade ruffs in hand. This is called RE-VERSING THE DUMMY.

South wins the spade lead, ruffs a spade, and can afford to test the trump situation by leading the ace of hearts and a heart to the 9. If it turned out that the trumps were 4–1 he would have to abandon the dummy reversal and rely on the club finesse. As it is, all players follow to two rounds of trumps.

South ruffs the third round of spades, crosses to the jack of diamonds, and ruffs the last spade. Then he enters dummy with the king of diamonds and uses the last heart in dummy to draw the outstanding trump. It is the mark of reverse dummy play that at the finish dummy has the long trump.

As all have followed to four rounds of spades, it is safe now to finesse the queen of clubs for an overtrick. The finesse loses but South makes the rest of the tricks.

66. Establishing a Suit by Ruffing

One of the most valuable uses of the trump suit is to establish a side suit by ruffing. At notrump not much can be done with a combination such as A x x x x opposite a singleton, but in a trump contract it is quite common for the declarer to establish the fifth round. Here the side suit is somewhat stronger:

```
              ♠ K J 4
              ♡ 10 7 5
              ◇ A 10 8 7 2
              ♣ A 3

  ♠ 10 5              N              ♠ 8 3
  ♡ K Q J 9                         ♡ A 8 2
  ◇ 6 3          W        E         ◇ Q J 9 5
  ♣ J 9 7 4 2        S              ♣ K 10 8 6

              ♠ A Q 9 7 6 2
              ♡ 6 4 3
              ◇ K 4
              ♣ Q 5
```

South plays in a contract of four spades. The defenders take the first three tricks in hearts and then West switches to a low club.

It is unlikely that West would have led a club from the king at this point, and as he has other chances South goes up with the ace. His general plan is to establish a winner in diamonds, on which his club loser can be discarded.

It would be a mistake to draw more than one round of trumps, because the trump suit may be needed for entry to the table. Declarer takes one round of spades with the ace, then plays the king and ace of diamonds, followed by a low diamond from dummy.

When East follows to the third diamond South has to decide whether to ruff low or with the queen. Since the contract will be safe if either trumps are 2–2 or diamonds 3–3, it is right for South to ruff with the queen, avoiding a possible overruff. When West shows out, South plays a spade to the jack, and his worries are over when both opponents follow suit. He leads a fourth diamond and ruffs, then enters dummy with the king of spades and cashes the fifth diamond, discarding the queen of clubs. His last card is a winning trump.

67. The Ruffing Finesse

Playing in a trump contract, the declarer is often able to finesse in a side suit against either opponent. Suppose he has a side suit such as:

A Q 10 9 8

J

He can take a straightforward finesse of the queen, but usually it will be a better play to lead the jack to the ace and return the queen, intending to discard a loser if the king does not appear. This is called a RUFFING FINESSE.

The ruffing finesse is often a form of safety play, as here:

```
                    ♠ A J 4
                    ♡ A K 10 9
                    ◇ 8 7 3
                    ♣ 7 4 2
  ♠ 9 6 5                              ♠ 10
  ♡ 8 4 2           ┌─────────┐       ♡ Q 6 5 3
  ◇ Q 10 6 4        │    N    │       ◇ K J 9 2
  ♣ A J 8           │ W     E │       ♣ Q 10 9 5
                    │    S    │
                    └─────────┘
                    ♠ K Q 8 7 3 2
                    ♡ J 7
                    ◇ A 5
                    ♣ K 6 3
```

South is in four spades and West leads a diamond. It
is often good play in a suit contract, as at notrump, to
hold up a control, but here South has other plans. He
wins with the ace of diamonds and plays the king of
spades, followed by a spade to the jack. He does not
play a third round, because he will need the ace of
spades for an entry. Instead, he plays off ace and king
of hearts, then leads the 10. If East covers with the
queen, South will ruff high and enter dummy with the
ace of spades to take a discard on the 9 of hearts.

If East plays low on the 10 of hearts, South will discard his diamond loser. It would not matter if West
were able to win with the queen, because the clubs
would be safe from attack and the ace of spades would
be an entry for the established 9 of hearts.

68. Retaining Trump Control

When the declarer plans to draw trumps and make
tricks in a side suit, he must be particularly careful not

to lose TRUMP CONTROL. That is to say, he must not let the situation arise where he cannot draw trumps and run his side suit. He may, however, leave the enemy in possession of a master trump. There are exceptions, but it is generally a mistake to play a round of trumps when an opponent holds the master.

```
                    ♠ 9 7 3 2
                    ♡ K 8 5
                    ◇ K Q 10
                    ♣ A Q 8

♠ K Q 10 5          ┌─────────┐          ♠ A J 8 4
♡ Q 9 6             │    N    │          ♡ 10 3
◇ A 8 5 2           │ W     E │          ◇ 7 4
♣ 9 7               │    S    │          ♣ J 10 6 4 3
                    └─────────┘
                    ♠ 6
                    ♡ A J 7 4 2
                    ◇ J 9 6 3
                    ♣ K 5 2
```

South is in four hearts and the defense begins with two rounds of spades.

On the surface, there are only three losers—one spade, one heart, and the ace of diamonds. But see what happens if South plays the hand "wide open."

After ruffing the second spade South leads a heart to the king and finesses the jack on the way back. West wins and "forces" again in spades. South must ruff and by this time he has only one trump left in his hand. He can draw the last trump and lead a diamond, but when West comes in with the ace of diamonds he will cash the fourth round of spades.

The opportunity to finesse in hearts was a lure that should have been resisted. A better percentage play is to cash king and ace of hearts, then force out the ace of diamonds. West will win, cash the queen of hearts, and lead another spade. South has a trump left, so he can ruff and make his winners in the minor suits.

Part VII

THE LANGUAGE OF DEFENSE

Defense is the most difficult part of the game, depending more on experience than technique. When you have played for a few months and have acquired the feel of the game, you will be able to profit from the chapters on defense in a comprehensive textbook.* We concentrate here on opening strategy and on signals and conventions that occur throughout the play.

*E.g. *The Complete Book of Bridge,* by Terence Reese and Albert Dormer.

69. The Opening Lead at Notrump

The opening lead is a problem in two parts: which suit to lead, and which card of that suit. The first is a matter of judgment, the second of convention.

Which suit to lead

We have already noted that the play at notrump usually develops into a struggle between the two sides to establish their long suits. Thus, in principle, the leader chooses his "longest and strongest suit." But that maxim is only half true: the real objective is to lead the longest and strongest suit held by the *partnership*.

These are some considerations that may deter you from leading your long suit:

• A shorter suit is more readily establishable. A lead from Q J 10 9 is obviously more promising than a lead from J x x x x.

• A lead from a holding such as A Q x x, A K x x, K Q x x is likely to cost a trick and does not possess the compensating advantage of developing a long suit. Against one notrump, especially, you should be inclined to play a safe, defensive game, letting the declarer find his own tricks.

• Your hand is so weak that it seems advisable to play for your partner's hand. For example, the bidding has gone one notrump—three notrump and you hold:

♠ K 7 4
♡ 8 5
◇ J 7 3
♣ 9 6 5 4 2

A club lead is unlikely to achieve anything. Any of the other suits might turn out a lucky choice, but on the whole a spade is best: it is a major suit, which the opponents have not thought it worth while to explore, and you are demanding less, in the sense that if partner holds, say, Q J x x x, you will have struck gold.

Other reasons why you may refrain from leading your longest suit are: it has been bid by the opponents; your partner has bid a suit, which may offer better prospects than your own suit; your partner has doubled the final contract. (For the significance of a double, see the end of this section.)

Which card to lead

You have decided which suit to lead. The next question is which card of that suit. Old-established conventions exist in this area and it is wise to observe them, because otherwise partner may draw a wrong conclusion.

When you hold a strong honor combination you must avoid giving the declarer a "cheap" trick. For example, it would be silly to lead low from K Q J x x, perhaps allowing the declarer to make two tricks with a holding no better than A 10 x. The general rule is to lead the TOP OF A SEQUENCE or the higher of TOUCHING HONORS, an exception being that the king is led from A K. (Some players treat the ace as a request to partner to drop his highest card.)

From a suit headed by:

A K Q lead K	Q J 9 lead Q
A K J lead K	J 10 9 lead J
A Q J lead Q	J 10 8 lead J
A Q 10 lead fourth best	A 10 9 lead 10
A J 10 lead J	K 10 9 lead 10
K Q J lead K	Q 10 9 lead 10
K Q 10 lead K	10 9 8 lead 10
Q J 10 lead Q	10 9 7 lead 10

Also lead the top card from any low sequence such as 9 8 7 x or 8 7 5 x. One reason is to warn partner that the suit is not headed by a high honor.

With combinations not containing three honors the conventional lead is the fourth best, the 5 from K 9 7 5, the 6 from A Q 8 6 4 2. The reason for leading low from a combination such as A K x x x is to leave partner with a card to play back when he gains the lead.

The lead from three to an honor

Lead the higher from touching honors, the queen from Q J x, but otherwise the low card. This applies equally when you are leading a suit bid by your partner. The advantage is seen if you imagine the distribution to be like this:

	(a) 5 4			(b) 6	
K 10 8		Q 9 7 3 2	J 8 4		A Q 9 7 3
	A J 6			K 10 5 2	

In these and countless other positions the lead of a high card will tend to give the declarer an unnecessary trick. By leading the 8 in (a) and the 4 in (b), you retain valuable cards over the declarer.

The lead from a short suit

It is usual to lead the top card from three small, but it must be said that some players prefer to lead the middle card from a combination such as 9 6 3. With any doubleton lead the top card, the 7 from 7 5, the queen from Q 4.

The lead when partner has doubled

A double of three notrump, or even two notrump, should generally be regarded as LEAD-DIRECTING. When the defending side has bid a suit, the double urges that this suit be led, with a preference for the leader's suit when both defenders have bid. When no suit has been bid by the defenders, the double asks for a lead of the first suit bid by dummy. A double "out of the blue" says: "Don't lead your best suit: try to find mine." A defender holding K Q J 10 x and a side entry may double in the hope that his partner will be able to find the killing lead.

70. The Opening Lead in a Suit Contract

At notrump, as we have seen, a player will often lead from a holding such as A Q x x x or K J x x x, knowing that he may be giving up an immediate trick but hoping to establish his suit. In a suit contract safety is more important. There is not much point in developing a suit if the declarer has enough trumps to ruff it.

There are times, however, when the bidding will suggest that an attacking lead is called for. For example, the bidding goes:

South	West	North	East
—	—	1 ◇	pass
1 ♡	pass	2 ◇	pass
3 ♡	pass	4 ♡	pass
pass	pass		

Now it is known that dummy has a good suit of diamonds. West must lead from the black suit that is more likely to develop early tricks. He should attack from K x x rather than from 9 8 7 x x, from Q x rather than from J 10 x x x.

Most of the conventions in leading are the same as at notrump. There are two exceptions: lead the higher card from touching honors, the king from K Q x x x, the queen from Q J x x, not fourth best; and if you must lead from a suit headed by an unsupported ace, lead the ace, not a low card.

There are certain tactical leads which occur only in a suit contract:

Short suit leads

A lead from a plain singleton or doubleton is relatively safe, in that you are not sacrificing an honor card, and it may lead to a ruff. The prospect of a ruff is always improved when you hold a trick in the trump suit, as you may then have a second opportunity to put your partner in the lead.

One caution: NEVER lead a singleton of a side suit bid by the declarer. You will warn him of the distribution and probably kill your partner's holding in the suit.

Forcing leads

The defenders are said to play a forcing game when they make the declarer shorten his trumps to the point at which he loses trump control. It is often possible to foresee when this type of defense will be effective. For example, South plays in four spades and West holds:

♠ Q 8 7 3
♡ K J 8 5 2
◇ 6 2
♣ A 8

If the bidding has suggested that the trumps are 4–4, a diamond may be the best and safest lead; but if the trumps are more likely to be 5–3, the policy of the defenders should be to gain trump control. West should lead from his long suit, hearts, intending to play this suit at every opportunity.

Trump leads

A trump lead from x x or x x x is safe and will sometimes prevent the declarer from playing a ruffing or crossruffing game. Nevertheless, it is not as a rule good policy to lead a trump unless there seems a positive reason for doing so. It takes experience to recognize such situations, but sometimes it will be apparent that the opponents have found a good fit in just one suit and will play to make their trumps separately.

A singleton trump is not a recommended lead, because of the danger of exposing partner's Q x x or J x x x.

The lead against a slam

An attacking lead from a king or a queen in an unbid suit is often best against a small slam. You hope to find partner with a corresponding honor and to establish a trick which you can cash if your side comes in later. Against a grand slam a safe lead, often a trump, is indicated.

The lead when a slam contract has been doubled

The double of a slam contract is specifically lead-directing. It asks the leader to find a *surprise* lead. The doubler may hold a void or A Q in a suit bid by the dummy.

71. The Play by Third Hand

While it is usual to *lead* the top card of a sequence, it is correct to play the *bottom* card.

7 4 2

K 10 8 5 3   Q J 6

A 9

West leads the 5, East plays the jack. If South takes the trick with the ace West will be able to place his partner with the queen, since with A Q declarer would presumably have won with the lower card.

There is a general rule, "second hand low, third hand high." Though there are many exceptions to both parts of this advice, it will serve as a warning against the error known as "finessing against partner."

7 5 3

Q 9 6 2   K 10 4

A J 8

When West leads the 2, East must not worry about contributing his king. To play the 10, obviously, would present declarer with an extra trick.

It is, however, perfectly correct to finesse against the *dummy* in positions of this kind:

(a)   J 7 4   (b)   Q 9 5

K 10 8 6 2   Q 9 5   J 8 6 4 2   K 10 7

A 3   A 3

Suppose that in (a) West leads the 6 and dummy plays low. East must finesse the 9. He is finessing against dummy's jack, not against his partner. In (b), when West leads the 4 and dummy plays the 5, East must finesse the 7 to be sure of holding South to one trick.

72. Defensive Signals and Conventions

The principle of leading fourth best applies throughout the defense. It is especially useful in this situation:

7

K J 6 4 2   A 9 5 3

Q 10 8

At notrump West leads the 4, East wins with the ace and returns the 3, his original fourth best. West captures the 10 with the jack and, placing his partner with four of the suit, can safely lay down the king. Note that, if the play goes like this, East must not fail to UNBLOCK the 9 on the third round.

An equally important inference may arise when the partner of the opening leader returns a card that is obviously not his fourth best. Suppose the distribution to be:

6

K J 7 5 2   A 8 4

Q 10 9 3

West leads the 5, East wins with the ace and returns the 8. South may cover with the 9, 10, or possibly the queen. In each case West, defending against a notrump contract, must realize that his partner holds only three cards and that declarer has a certain stopper. If West has a quick side entry he may win and clear the suit, but if he lacks a quick entry he must play low. Then, if East obtains the lead later on, he will have a card to return and West will take three more winners. We have here an example of ducking play in defense. It is worth bearing in mind that the mechanics of the game are just the same for the defenders as they are for the declarer.

Signals to show encouragement

An unnecessarily high card, usually a 7 or better, played on partner's lead, or when discarding on declarer's lead of a different suit, is an encouraging signal. An ECHO, or HIGH-LOW, such as the 4 followed by the 2, has a similar implication.

Signals to show distribution

When it is apparent that the signal cannot relate to strength, an echo signifies an *even* number of cards. For example, partner leads the king from A K x x x against a suit contract, and you hold 6 3. You play high-low to show that you can ruff the third round.

A special convention attaches to the trump suit. A "trump echo" denotes precisely *three* (or five) cards in the trump suit.

Distributional signals are vital when declarer is developing a long suit in a dummy which is short of entries:

KQJ75

9 4 2   A 8 6

10 3

South leads the 10, which holds the first trick. West's play of the 2 followed by the 4 tells East that he holds an odd number, so East can count 13 and safely win the second round.

LAWS AND PROPRIETIES

The full code of Laws amounts to more than half the present book in length and does not lend itself to abbreviation. A player who is learning the game need not concern himself with the Laws but should in time familiarize himself with the procedure relating to common infringements such as Insufficient Bid, Pass or Bid out of Turn, Lead or Play out of Turn, and Revoke.

The Proprieties are not always self-evident. Briefly, it is entirely fair to:

• Exact the legal penalty for an infringement, even when no damage has been suffered.
• Warn partner against committing an irregularity.
• Maintain silence about an offense committed by one's own side; but it is wrong to take any abnormal action to conceal it, and wrong to commit any offense deliberately.
• Depart from an announced convention. If you pass a forcing bid or give the "wrong" response to Blackwood, only your partner can complain.

• Act on an inference drawn from an opponent's hesitation or remark; but you do so at your own risk and have no redress if it turns out you were mistaken.

It is unfair, or at best improper, to:

• Draw attention to the score (after the deal has been completed) or to the number of tricks won or lost during the play.
• Attempt to mislead an opponent by any remark, gesture, grimace, or avoidable hesitation.
• Call or play with special emphasis, or act in any way (as by indicating displeasure) likely to convey information to partner.
• Be influenced in any way by partner's remark, hesitation or manner (for example, a "quick double" or "slow pass"). This is often difficult; a player must "lean over backwards" to make it clear that he has not drawn any inference to which he was not justly entitled.

SCORING TABLE

Score below the line for tricks bid and made:

Spades or hearts	30 per trick
Diamonds or clubs	20 per trick
Notrump	40 for first trick, 30 for each additional trick

If the contract has been doubled, multiply the trick score by 2; if redoubled, by 4.

100 points below the line wins game, but no separate score is recorded until the rubber has been won.

Score above the line:

Overtricks

	Not vulnerable	*Vulnerable*
Undoubled	Ordinary trick value	Ordinary trick value
Doubled	100 per trick	200 per trick
Redoubled	200 per trick	400 per trick

Making double or redouble contract:
In addition to all other scores: 50.

Honors

4 trump honors in any one hand	100
5 trump honors in any one hand	150
4 aces in one hand at notrump	150

Slam bonuses

Small slam not vulnerable 500, vulnerable 750.
Grand slam not vulnerable 1000, vulnerable 1500.

Penalties for undertricks

	Not vulnerable	*Vulnerable*
Undoubled	50 each trick	100 each trick
Doubled	100 for first trick, 200 for each additional trick	200 for first trick, 300 for each additional trick
Redoubled	Twice the above	Twice the above

Rubber bonus

When the rubber is won in two games: 700
When the rubber is won by two games to one: 500

Unfinished rubber

Bonus for a side that is a game ahead: 300
Bonus for a part score in an unfinished game: 50

INDEX

Other SIGNET and MENTOR Books
for Your Reference Shelf

**Buy them at your local
bookstore or use coupon
on next page for ordering.**

More MENTOR and SIGNET Reference Books